TALENT IS JUST THE BEGINNING

an artists' guide to marketing in the 21st Century

Bette Ridgeway

Aardvark Global Publishing, LLC
Salt Lake City, UT

ISBN: 978-1-4276-3779-6

Printed in the United States of America

Cover design by Bette Ridgeway
www.ridgewaystudio.com

For Stephen

Table of Contents

Acknowledgements

I am deeply grateful to those who have encouraged and inspired me over the years--most especially my wonderful sons, Scott, Greg and Matthew.

Thanks also to Don Davenport and Annette Hayden for their editorial guidance and to Anabele Ferguson for her contribution to the section on alternative spaces.

"You have brains in your head
You have feet in your shoes
You can steer yourself
Any direction you choose."

Dr. Seuss

INTRODUCTION

Scores of books have been written on the business of art, but none has addressed the unique challenges facing the art world in 2009. Just as financial advisor and author, Suze Orman is calling upon us to "wake up" and get involved in our financial futures, I am calling upon artists to do their homework in order to keep their careers on the pathway to success. Business as usual will no longer work!

We are dealing with a new and more complex set of challenges facing the global art marketplace. As most businesses are looking at ways to cut costs and maximize their position to make a profit, artists also are finding ways to purchase supplies in bulk, setting up informal, inexpensive figure-drawing classes, identifying ways to creatively engage their collectors, while utilizing the global reach of the Internet to advance their art careers.

The days of the artist working at his/her easel with assistants scurrying around cleaning brushes, sweeping floors, washing coffee cups and answering phone calls from dealers, managers and eager collectors are nearly extinct. Only a handful of artists reach this level of success, and bravo to them!

Most of us would rather spend our time creating our art and evolving our artistic talents. Purists would claim that the notion of "business" in the visual arts may draw criticism. Times have changed, however, requiring artists to employ their imaginations not only in their work, but also in how to make a living at it.

I am often asked, "What makes an artist a professional?" My reply is the following: "When you put a price tag on your artwork, you have determined that you wish to sell it. That makes you a professional." I have a friend who is an expert seamstress. She charges a fee for her work. That makes her a professional seamstress. This is no longer a hobby for her, nor is it a hobby for artists who sell their work.

There are pros and cons to this, obviously! If you are a professional artist who is in business, striving to make a profit, then certain expenses that you accrue toward the selling of your "product" are tax deductible. Therefore, it is mandatory that you become proficient in the business of being in the art business. What is deductible? How do I devise a simple inventory system? When do I need to invest in a website? What are the tax laws pertaining to artists?

Those artists who are not dependent upon selling their work do not have to worry about such things. Those of us who are growing our art business can only profit by being aware of the rules and using them to our advantage.

My intention with this book is to reach out to artists who are eager to develop their business skills. Some of the topics include finding and dealing with galleries, pricing artwork, portfolios, photos, mailing lists, finding alternative venues in which to sell, websites, tax issues and more! Dealing efficiently with your business will actually create more time for you in the studio - *and* you will sleep better.

The plan is to update the material every couple of years. Your input is appreciated and I look forward to providing some serious in formation and some serious inspiration!

Bette Ridgeway
Santa Fe, NM
March 2009

"I have no special talents.
I am only passionately curious."

Albert Einstein

"Talent is God-given;
success must be earned."

B. Ridgeway

What is talent, anyway?

Since the beginning of time, scholars have been trying to define talent. When I think of talent, I think of ***teachability*** and ***learnability***. Yes, learning is a lifelong process, as artists have demonstrated since recorded history.

Practicing artists are constantly evolving, growing and exploring new ways in which to express themselves. With so many choices today, we are always trying new types of paint or finishes. Surfaces are no longer just canvas and paper; artists are using plexiglas, metal and any number of interesting grounds. Artists, and particularly those artists who are successful, possess a high level of "learnability."

When researching the definition of "talent" it is interesting to see the range of material written on the subject. Before making this investigation, I was convinced that talents were skills by another name. However, the consensus of opinion suggests that a critical difference is that skills are acquired abilities whereas talents are natural abilities.

Talents, I have come to realize, are just like skills, they need to be identified, encouraged, nourished and developed. And, despite all evidence to the contrary, I still believe that a so-called 'natural' talent only predisposes people to do something well, and, left to its own devises, starved of the opportunity to flourish, it could lie dormant and fail to materialize.

Leonardo da Vinci had unparalleled talent, but what set him apart was his desire to find answers. His journals reflect a mind that never stopped looking and learning. Many artists produce sketchbooks that go beyond their art.

One of Leonardo's notebooks written between 1506–1510 was purchased by Microsoft's Bill Gates in 1994. Gates had been fascinated by da Vinci's work since he was a boy. An astonishing painter and sculptor, the artist was a genius in more fields than any scientist and filled his notebooks with questions, concepts, challenges and explanations.

As he developed his artistic talents, his writings included observations about light and the phenomenon of how light is reflected off paint.

He also observed, "Iron rusts from disuse, stagnant water loses purity and in cold weather becomes frozen; even so does inaction sap the vigor of the mind." Leonardo was learning his entire life. His curiosity was a passion.

Picasso also had a deep curiosity. His 178 sketchbooks contained not only studies for exploring themes and compositions, but also reflected a very fertile mind and the depth of his thought process.

So, if we have some idea what talent it, then how does it translate to success? Character, self-discipline and integrity come to mind. We all know many talented individuals who just don't have the discipline to make it in the competitive marketplace. They have difficulty in completing a painting, framing it, naming it, photographing it, putting it into a show and selling it.

It is sad because so many of these people are enormously talented. But, *talent* is just the BEGINNING.

Strength of character helps to protect the talent. Conversely, the absence of strong character eventually topples talent. We see so many young, talented actors, musicians and artists self-destruct before fully developing their talent. What is the missing link?

When you look at an iceberg, on average 15% is visible. This represents talent. The unseen 85% below the surface is character.

The greater the talent, the greater the need for a strong character to sustain that talent.

Sometimes, as history has shown, those who are "top-heavy" with talent are likely to have self-destructive tendencies. In the visual arts, there are many very talented artists who have left us too soon, as their character did not support their talent.

Helen Keller, author and activist, who could neither hear nor see, said, "Character cannot be developed in ease and quiet. Only through experience of trial and suffering can the soul be strengthened, vision cleared, ambition inspired and success achieved."

What, you may ask, does all this have to do with marketing? I would say that it goes to the very heart of what artists do. We create art, and, if we have the requisite strength of character, we can learn the skills necessary to be successful. If that is our goal, then we can reach it. The decision is ours!

We artists do have control of how our work is presented, priced, photographed and viewed. While marketing is often considered the most challenging aspect of being an artist, it can also provide the most rewarding component of our creative lives.

Character protects your talent.
Practice develops your talent.
Talent+Character+Practice is a
winning combination.

One of the paradoxes of life is that things that initially make you successful are not always the things that keep you successful."

- Unknown

"I value artists who embody the expression of their life.

Wassily Kandinsky

CHAPTER I

A New Reality

This does not come as a news flash: The state of the art market in 2009 is unpredictable. The general economy as well as the art economy is headed for choppy waters. The affects of the credit crunch is also impacting the marketplace as well. Today a different reality prevails.

Pace Wildenstein, one of the most prominent galleries in New York laid off 18 employees in January. "The luxury of carrying underperforming employees is now a thing of the past," wrote Larry Gagosian in a memo to his staff.

Sotheby's is also trimming its workforce, and has announced it has abandoned guarantees for the foreseeable future. The firm, and its arch-rival Christie's, were badly hit by the collapse in art prices during New York's sales of impressionist, modern and contemporary art in November 2008, which garnered only half the expected totals. Those sales were designated before the autumn, when art prices were still riding high. Some works sold in November for half their low estimates, and up to 75% of the works in same sales were achieved.

The lackluster 2008 autumn art fairs, Frieze and Art Basel Miami Beach, saw dealers prepared to be flexible on prices, accepting discounts of up to 30%, but as journalist, sociologist and lecturer Andras Szanto points out: "Just as designer brands are now being offered at huge discounts–were those shoes or handbags really worth the previous price?

Those pre-financial meltdown prices should never have been so huge. Some dealers priced art so aggressively, and the prices went up with such velocity, that it is inevitable that they should fall back sharply."

The Auction Houses

Art + Auction Magazine, which has its fingers on the pulse of auction buying and selling, reported in its January 09 issue that the party is over in the market for American paintings. In December, the 184 lots offered by Sotheby's in the category brought in roughly $25 million, while the 186 at Christie's grossed a mere $20 million. Those totals, a fraction of the sums the houses achieved in May, are the lowest they have generated in at least five years.

According to Dara Mitchell, the executive vice president and director of the American-paintings department at Sotheby's, the market is recalibrating. 'It is perceptibly different from a year ago. In this sale there was resistance to current prices at every level, even though the estimates were down by 20 percent. Clients expected to buy things under the low estimate, like at luxury department stores where everything is on sale.'

But some bidders were still brave enough to put up significant sums. At Sotheby's, five of the top 10 lots sold for more than $1 million. The highest price was for *Sunrise at Tappan Zee,* 1874 (est. $1.5-2 million), a luminous painting of the Hudson River by

Francis A. Silva, which an American collector bought for a record $2,658,500. Two other lots that were estimated to be worthy of multimillion-dollar prices, Georgia O'Keeffe's *Blue Wave Maine,* 1926 (est. $1.5-2.5 million), and Marsden Hartley's *The Silence of High Noon,* circa 1908 (est. $1.5-2.5 million), wound up selling just above their low estimates.

Museums were also going after top-tier works. An unidentified U.S. institution purchased Stuart Davis's *Still Life with Map, New Mexico,* 1923 (est. $1.5-2.5 million), for $1,538,500. And the Princeton University Art Museum stretched to win Robert Walter Weir's 1833 painting *Greenwich Boat Club* (est. $400-600,000), which depicts a group of artists seeking respite outside New York during the city's cholera epidemic of 1832, for an artist's record of $1.2 million.

For the most part, however, "the air thinned out at prices over $1 million and even more over $2 million. There wasn't a lot of froth or loft," says Mitchell. She also points out that there was very little dealer participation for paintings over $200,000. "People are very selective now. Things that would have sold last year didn't," says the Connecticut dealer Thomas Colville, who found several of the estimates too high.

"The liveliest section of the sale was the modern material," says the department head Eric Widing, noting that there may be a trend away from classic, academic 19th-Century genre painting. Such a shift would help explain why Winslow Homer's 1887 watercolor *After the Rain, Prouts Neck* (est. $2.5-3.5 million) – the most heavily publicized and steeply estimated lot of the sale – passed at $1.7 million. "But," he adds, "there is still broad interest in the other categories: modern, Ashcan School, the New Hope Circle, Western works, Hudson River and Impressionism."

So at the beginning of 2009, what are the prospects for the art market? As long as we see wild fluctuations on Wall Street, people will not be spending a lot of money on art.

The Upside

There is an upside to this, thankfully. 2009 is the perfect year to take advantage of the record instability of the financial markets. It is a collector's market now. Therefore, there is a mandate to artists: Marketing is more important than ever. It is up to us to reach out to potential clients and to nurture those who have purchased our work in the past. The target is existing collectors. They have a stake, as they want to see us succeed.

Another positive is our new president, Barak Obama. Unlike most American presidents, he writes his own books. He is said to enjoy music, especially blues and jazz. His chief of staff is a former ballet dancer. His appointees have enough Ph.ds to fill a football stadium. But what will his arts policy be and what will it mean for the visual arts? Hopes are for an administration that is not only more progressive, but also smarter.

This could be good news for the arts–as long as we can build a convincing case that the arts serve the public interest. We have been given positive indicators such as the Obama-Biden "Platform in Support for the Arts," which, by virtue of its existence, is an extraordinary document. It was also unusually specific: invest in arts education, expand public/private partnerships between schools and arts organizations, create an "Artist Corps" to work in low-income schools and communities, increase funding for the National Endowment for the Arts (NEA) and promote cultural diplomacy. There is every reason to believe these priorities should outlast the campaign.

Another widely anticipated change has to do with the mechanics of government support. Total cultural expenditures by the federal government–through agencies for education, parks, transportation, trade and even defense–vastly exceed the NEA's paltry budget. (Compare the NEA's $144M annual allocation to the $10 billion Obama has pledged for early childhood education.) Rather than try to massively boost the NEA–a hard sell, even in the best of times – the administration will likely emphasize coordination across the full breadth of government.

No "arts czar" is likely to be installed in the West Wing, and my bet is that calls to create a cabinet-level "Secretary of the Arts" (a petition initiated by musician and music producer, Quincy Jones, that most of us signed,) will fall on deaf ears.

Unfortunately, the arts will be at the back of the line of potential bailout targets. Every museum, university, cultural group, symphony and ballet company is composing its own wish list. Surely, we will hear pleas to revive Depression-era programs in art, music and theater. If government could employ 3,700 visual artists in 1933-34, the thinking goes, why not do the same in our current hour of need?

We can be warmed by the fact that Obama, in his biography, wrote about his Mother's love of the paintings of Cezanne and the time spent at the Metropolitan Museum with her. This is a man who knows art, understands contemporary art and likes it. How this translates into policy remains to be seen.

The Future

While we all understand that the economy will eventually turn around, we must survive in the interim and plan for the future.

There are some avenues for selling artwork that remain reasonably strong. Where are they? What venues are they? What is selling? Art dealers representing the "blue-chip artists" continue to thrive, *but* they are working harder. Collectors in this lofty arena are being more cautious about making big expenditures, so dealers are being kept on their toes to generate business.

In addition, competition has never been greater. Our nation's 280 accredited schools of art are turning out thousands of talented graduates who are entering the marketplace each year with fresh ideas and dreams of a meaningful career. The Bureau of Labor Statistics (BLS) documents the trends in the art markets which indicate huge growth in the areas of graphic design and animation. Technology is labeled the single-greatest contributor to changes in the art industry.

The BLS reports that the employment of artists is projected to grow faster than average. Competition for jobs is expected to be keen for both salaried and freelance jobs in all the specialties because the number of people with creative ability and an interest in pursuing this career is expected to continue to exceed the number of available openings.

Despite the competition, employers and individual clients are always on the lookout for creative artists. Employment of artists and related workers is expected to grow 16 percent through 2016, faster than the average for all occupations.

Economic and technical changes have also moved New York City out of the forefront of the art industry. An increasingly high cost of living has turned off many budding artists, and, because scanners, software and the Internet allow the real-time sharing of artwork, it is no longer necessary for artists to be physically present in New York City to market their work. While still the center of the commercial art industry, it is no longer the place to move to when launching an art career.

Now, more than ever, it is very important to study and assimilate the business of art. No longer can we just float along on the raft of past success. We must be pro-active in deliberately attracting collectors, resources, networks and all means of support to keep us going.

The successful artist in business spends 50% percent (yes!) of his/her time on marketing. We would much rather be at the easel, but the truth is there is no alternative.

Obviously, if you are already famous and have a staff of public relations people and assistants, you have already achieved success. Odds are, you did spend a large amount of your time promoting yourself and your work in order to achieve this success.

For most of us, however, are somewhere between the street-fair artists and the wildly successful internationally-recognized artists. We have become relatively adept at creating our artwork. Now, we are becoming more serious about how to get it out there and sell it.

Look around at the artists you know that are making a living. How are they different from you? What makes them successful? Are they business oriented? Are they able to shamelessly self-promote? I'm not joking here. We all know artists whose work is not so great who are successful, as well as those who create incredible work and struggle to make a living.

Let's go a little deeper. What does it mean to be successful as an artist? The answer might be something like this: The successful artist is able to create a reasonable amount of artwork that is placed in venues that generate an income that not only pays for the art supplies, but also the travel, the advertising, the printing, the website and perhaps put food on the table.

Each of us has our own view of what success means to us. The definition changes as we mature and become more known.

Can we assume that most of us wish to be acknowledged as competent artists? Winning some acclaim in competitions can move our careers forward. Making deposits to our bank account also rewards us.

We all need to develop the skills to advance our careers so that we can make those deposits regularly! During these challenging times we have no choice but to investigate what I call, "New Opportunities."

New Opportunities

The most important of these is the Internet. There is no tool more important to master at this time in our evolution. The Internet has opened up a world of opportunity not only for fine artists to put their work before a global audience, but also to freelance graphic artists who use the myriad of job posting websites to find new work.

In 1966, through the combined efforts of the Defense Advanced Research Project Agency (DARPA, formed in 1958), the National Physics Network in the UK and CYCLADES a French Science Organization, the beginnings of the World Wide Web were formed for scientific, military and commercial applications.

Designed by Tim Berners-Lee, a French engineer for the Council European Research Nuclear (CERN), The World Wide Web went public in 1993. (If you study the history of the internet, Al Gore's name is never mentioned.)

Since the Web went public, the increase in the numbers of new websites being created each year is staggering. In August of 1995 there were only 18,000 websites created. In 2007 the number rose to 107,000,000. This rate of growth is expected to continue for many years to come.

The world of the Internet is impacting all businesses and artists are no exception. We have changed the ways in which we advertise our business, as well.

Have you noticed how the search function has improved over the last couple of years? Now you can type almost anything in Google and dozens of pieces of information and websites will be listed. You can type a barcode into the Google search bar from a food item and get information on its ingredients immediately. This instantaneous access to information affects the way we not only get information but also the way we do business, globally.

Sales and rentals of art instruction material are booming also. www.ccpvideos.com an outstanding online resource for purchasing videos has added a streaming component, so subscribers will be able to watch the videos and DVDs at home instantly. With online previews available, purchasing decisions are easily made.

In the online commercial world, it is heartening to know that Amazon logged the best holiday season in 2008 despite the rough economy.

Amazon's CEO Jeff Bezos says, "There are two ways to extend your business. ***Take inventory of what you're good at and extend out from your skills***. Or determine what your customers want and work backward, even if it means learning new skills." We can all benefit from this.

For artists, we need to analyze what is selling. If our landscapes are selling and there are no portrait commissions in the works, where do we spend our energy?

Think about how you can utilize the web. How can you reach out to new collectors? What are people looking for on the web? How can you maximize this amazing tool?

Digital Cameras

Second in importance is the digital camera. Digital cameras are affordable and their use can be mastered in a couple of weeks or less. We cannot be dependent upon our kids or our friends to take good photos of our work.

If you can afford a professional photographer, I applaud you. However, I must ask, what happens when there is a photography emergency? For example, you have received an important request for an image that is new and available but ***not yet*** photographed. How will you deal with this? Collectors and galleries sometimes have a short attention span, and we must react in a timely fashion for requests such as these.

Bottom line: *you* must take control of your photographs. And, you must be able to email them! Fortunately, this is no longer a mystery. *Now* is the time to push forward. If you have already done this, congratulations!

Every work of art must be photographed for a variety of uses. Galleries want high resolution images for advertising purposes, and websites require a smaller, compressed format.

I remember a conversation in 1988 with my friend and mentor, Paul Jenkins. We met at his NY gallery prior to a big show. We sat together in the back office, and I was filled with questions about his new work, which was massive and exciting. Instead, he steered the conversation to photographs.

He was working on a book of his artwork and was frustrated that many images of his earlier work were dismal or non existent. He made me promise to get good photos of everything. Good advice, which I continue to follow to this very day!

I strongly urge you to master photographing your own work. That is not to say that if you are being considered for a major show you should hesitate to have it professionally photographed. Yes, engage the skills of a first-rate photographer for this.

If you do not already have a high-quality digital camera there are many resources online to compare all the options. www.dcresource.com is just one helpful resource.

Plus, there are many books to help you in photographing your work. In Lee Caplin's book, "The Business of Art," there is an entire chapter devoted to this.

Online resources:

http://www.theartistsweb.net/wiki/How_To_Photograph_Artwork

This writer advocates a two-step approach. One is a simple and cheap; requiring only a camera and a tripod, the other is a more complex approach requiring the use of professional-level equipment.

Most important, the artwork must be square with the camera. The center of the lens should be focused directly at the center of the artwork, whether it is horizontal or vertical in format. Don't use a wide-angle lens as it will distort the image. Shooting in natural daylight will give you great results. This does not mean shooting in the sun – an overcast day at midday works well.

http://www.vividlight.com/articles/1713.htm

Mark D. Thellmann gives sound advice regarding the creation of top quality slides to document their creations, gain access to juried shows, and produce printed promotional pieces. He discusses the kind of camera that can produce quality slides leading to shows and sales.

http://www.artlinkswap.org/photographing_art.shtml

This link has a short tutorial on how to take good photos of your artwork.

http://www.hawkinsonphotography.com/photo_art.html

As a service to the art community, Hawkinson Photography has produced a beginner's online guide to photographing art. The information is broken down into equipment, film, setup and techniques.

http://www.dallasartsrevue.com/resources/How-to-Photo-Art.shtml

J.R. Compton has a wonderful tutorial on shooting 2 and 3 dimensional artwork. We are reminded to be sure that our computer monitor is color calibrated so that we are viewing the colors accurately. The writer also discusses adjustable white balance settings.

http://www.bermangraphics.com/artshows/photographart.htm

Berman has details on shooting with a digital camera. Excellent information.

http://artdeadline.com

If you choose to join at $24 per year, you will get a free download "How to Photograph your Paintings" by Susan C. Cooper

"The artist is nothing without the gift,
but the gift is nothing without the work."

Emile Zola

"Creativity takes courage."

Henri Matisse

"You get whatever accomplishment
you are willing to declare."

Georgia O'Keeffe

CHAPTER 2

The Business of Art

It is fascinating to observe how the general public perceives artists. As an exercise, I suggest you begin to notice how people perceive you as you go through your daily routine.

For instance, at a dinner party when meeting new people, the conversation inevitably turns to, "So, what do you do?" When we say we are artists, what kind of response do we receive? Are we asked about our artwork, our upcoming exhibitions, our business, our clientele?

The point of this is to spark some interest in noticing the way in which we artists are perceived as others and to think about how ***you*** would like to be perceived by others.

The Artist as Business Person

An artist becomes a business person when a price tag goes up next to the artwork! It is validated when that first sale is made.

I like to say I am a "practicing" artist. Like an attorney who practices or a doctor who practices. It has a more weighty sound.

So, as practicing professionals, what are our priorities? Your personal list might look something like this:

Behave as an artist in business
Create an outstanding portfolio (hard & digital)
Find place(s) to show & sell our work
Set up record-keeping system for income & expense
Create an accurate inventory system
Establish consistent prices
Write a bio and statement
Develop an ad campaign
Create an artful website
Get into free directories
Understand copyright & trademark
Understand consignment laws

If we can become proficient at the above, we will be positioned to make a living.

What is your most important asset?

When I ask artists, they nearly always answer, "My talent." Yes, of course your talent is important, but talent is something that you have nurtured and developed over time. Remember, talent is just the beginning.

In my view, the most important possession - one which is uniquely yours and can never be taken from you - is your **name.**

When you think about famous artists, you immediately see, in your mind's eye, artist's work. Think about Picasso, Pollack, Van Gogh, and others. What do you see? I'll bet you can describe their work in some detail. It defines them!

Let's admit it, we would all like to have a name in the art world and be remembered long after we are gone.

So, accepting this premise, how do we market ourselves? How do we promote our artwork? How do we brand ourselves?

Branding

For me, "branding" simply means that when people hear your name, they can see your work in their mind's eye.

I love the story of Ralph Lauren whose birth name was Ralph Lipschitz. Born in the Bronx, New York, in 1939, Lauren grew up in a working-class neighborhood.

He did not attend fashion school, but worked for Brooks Brothers as a salesman. While selling ties at Brooks Brothers, he studied business at night school. It may well have been during his sales stint at Brooks Brothers, the conservative stylish menswear store, that Lauren met the "muse of tradition" which would earn him a formidable position in fashion history. In 1967, with the financial backing of Norman Hilton, Lauren opened a necktie store where he also sold ties of his own design, under the label "Polo". He later purchased the name from Hilton. Lauren has since grown his fashion empire into a billion-dollar business.

We have all witnessed the incredible expansion of Ralph Lauren's empire over the last 40 years. The company's merchandise, which falls into the categories of apparel, home products, accessories, fragrances and now paint, are marketed under a variety of brand names.

These include Polo, Polo by Ralph Lauren, Ralph Lauren Purple Label, Polo Sport, Ralph Lauren, RALPH, Lauren, Polo Jeans Co., RL, Chaps, and Club Monaco.

Women's Wear Daily synopsized Lauren's offerings as products that "portray a rugged romance and timeless elegance," and "present the seamless front of a wealthy, adventurous lifestyle." Bottom line: Lauren was able to create an image for himself and his products that reflected the needs of his buying public.

I'm not suggesting that artists should go to extremes in the branding business; however it is instructive to observe how others have achieved success in doing so.

Do you have an image? What is your signature? Is there a theme that runs through your artwork? What do people think of when they hear *your* name?

I implore every artist to think about ***how*** they wish to be perceived, not only as an artist, but also as a person who is in business to sell art. It is not difficult to accomplish a distinctive look to your materials. Get some help if necessary!

Corporate Art

There are several million works of art on display in corporations around the world, almost as many as are displayed in city art museums.

The value of the artworks housed and displayed in corporate offices is worth several billion dollars, and corporations spend millions every year purchasing art.

It is a fact that the most important patron of the arts during the last 50 years has been: not government, private collectors, religious groups or even museums, but corporations, internationally.

If you follow news of the business world, you've surely noticed how fast the corporate and business world changes, which also means that corporate art collections change as well. During the last two years there have been extensive changes--new collections appearing, some companies merging with others, some collections sold, and some companies disappearing completely.

While the current economy has certainly placed some constraints on the acquisition of new art for some corporations, there are still many opportunities. Hotels, in particular continue to expand their operations into Dubai, Singapore, China, Malaysia and more. The Bellagio in Las Vegas is a fine example of a corporate/ hospitality setting that includes a museum and art gallery.

An artist in business may want to know which companies have art collections, which corporations have commissioned art, which companies have planned art education programs, and which companies have sponsored art exhibitions or loaned their collections.

You can find answers in the International Directory of Corporate Art Collections. Since 1983, the International Art Alliance has published this valuable tool. Currently, the artist's edition, which comes on a CD, costs $78.50 plus $3.50 shipping.

Check out this gold mine of information: www.humanities-exchange.org

More Resources for the Artist in Business

Art Calendar Magazine

This is the industry's foremost business magazine for visual artists. Founded in 1986, *Art Calendar* acts as a beacon to guide artists on their journey toward making a living with their art.

Written by knowledgeable industry pros and successful working artists, *Art Calendar* offers artists practical business advice on subjects such as art marketing, art law, portfolio development, exhibition presentation, communication skills and sales techniques, as well as advanced technical applications of photography, computer and Web tools.

It also offers the most extensive and recent listings of Calls to Artists, including galleries reviewing portfolios, juried competitions, grants, fellowships, festivals, publishing opportunities and residencies.

Best described as "The Artist's Guide to Making It," ***Art Calendar*** is the only subscription-driven, business-oriented magazine published specifically for visual artists.

There are no "how-to-paint" articles – ***Art Calendar*** readers have already found their voice and established their own unique style.

Art Calendar enables professional artists to make a living doing what they love, providing them with fresh and innovative ideas, along with the all of the necessary tools to sell their work and further their careers. Offering professional artists more useful resources than any other art publication, in my estimation, ***Art Calendar*** has established itself as the ultimate resource for visual artists.

You can also subscribe to an online version. Check out their website: http://www.artcalendar.com

There are many organizations–local, regional and national which support the efforts of visual artists.

On the national level, the **Alliance for Professional Artists** (APA) is committed to supporting and educating art-driven individuals and groups, while serving as an advocate for the art community.

Members consist of individual artists, art schools, museums, galleries, studios, art organizations, communities, associations, foundations and more.

APA is aware of the challenges existing in the artist environment and serves as a support resource by offering healthcare discounts, merchandise and product discounts, a venue for open communication with other members, a vehicle to showcase their work, an e-commerce site to sell their work and other special pricing opportunities for members only.

In addition to supporting the artist community, APA endeavors to serve as an education resource. APA offers members numerous tools to grow as artists. All members receive a subscription to *Art Calendar,* an informative business magazine for visual artists. Resources also include sample resumes, artist statements, consignment contracts, educational webinars and a monthly e-newsletter providing the most up-to-date income opportunities available and current industry news.

The APA also strives to serve as an advocate for artist rights, providing members with a platform to voice their opinions and solutions to current art issues.

Member programs include **medical plans, online Web seminars, art supply discounts and credit card processing programs**. Visit them at: www.allproartists.org

Art Business News (ABN) is the source for industry news, marketing issues and emerging trends that drive sales for art publishers, art galleries. With a strong focus on the art publishing industry, a monthly "Emerging Artists" section provides great exposure for up-and-coming artists.

This monthly magazine features art-related articles and interviews with and about artists and gallerists on the national level. International Art Fairs and Expos advertise and provide information about their events in ABN. http:// www.artbusinessnews.com

The Artist Help Network is a free information service designed to help artists take control of their careers. The network assists artists in locating information, resources, guidance and advice on a comprehensive range of career-related topics. The network focuses primarily on subjects of interest to fine artists. People working in the applied arts, arts administration and arts-related fields will also find this site useful.

The Artist Help Network is produced by Caroll Michels, a career coach, artist advocate and author of How to Survive & Prosper as an Artist (Henry Holt & Company, New York).

The site is organized to help you locate information that impacts your career now – and in the future. It is divided into seven general categories: Career, Exhibitions, Commissions & Sales, Money, Presentation Tools, Legal, and Other Resources. Each general category unfolds into numerous sub-topics offering an abundance of regional, national and international resources.

Listings include publications, organizations, professionals, Web sites, audio-visual materials, and software programs. http://www.theartisthelpnetwork.com

Artists Registry.com in an International community of Visual and Performing Artists. They connect artists together with galleries, museums and arts organizations, as well as placing your artwork before the eyes of thousands of art collectors worldwide.

Their website www.artistsregistry.com provides portfolios of artwork along with listings of artists, galleries, museums and art organizations. A message board features upcoming events and discussions about art and artists. There is a weekly email newsletter of current events and member activities.

"It is through art and through art only,
that we realize our perfection."

Oscar Wilde

"Art is like politics;
it is all about
perception."

B. Ridgeway

CHAPTER 3

Galleries & Alternative Spaces

I like to think of the gallery system as a pyramid. At the top are the very exclusive, high-end, established galleries that have been around for decades and handle only well-known, blue-chip artists. They also handle the estates of deceased artists. The crème-de-la-crème of the art gallery world, this is where artists dream of being represented.

New York, still the brightest constellation of the US art market, continues to glitter. Galleries are not limited to storefronts, but inhabit larger spaces of multistory garages, warehouses. When we think of the top of the pyramid, we think of the Marlborough Gallery, Gagosian, Pace Wildenstein, Mary Boone, Paula Cooper and other heavy hitters. Browse *Art News Magazine, Art in America, Art* and *Antiques*, etc, to see who is where.

Some of the living artists that we see in these galleries are Helen Frankenthaler, Paul Jenkins, Jim Dine, Brice Marden, Ed Moses and Richard Serra, among others. They also represent the estates of deceased artists such as Morris Louis, Robert Motherwell, Robert Rauschenberg, Joan Mitchell and Richard Diebenkorn.

Now, let's move downward to the middle area of the pyramid. Notice how the shape is wider, encompassing a larger percentage of the gallery spectrum. These are the galleries that are somewhere in the middle, to which we can more realistically aspire! These mid-range galleries are more accessible to the average collector and show exceptional original paintings, sculpture and limited editions.

Most offer art consulting services. (More on art consultants in Chapter 4)

In the area of realism, there are several wonderful galleries that come to mind, such as the Forum with spaces in both NYC and Los Angeles, and Arcadia in NYC.

At the bottom and widest area of the pyramid are those galleries that we see in greater numbers throughout the US. These are the galleries we see in malls, large and small. They feature some original work, but mostly multiples that are affordable to the masses. Many of these galleries sell posters and also have a frame shop.

There are exceptional galleries in this category that may carry licensed artwork by well-known or emerging artists. An example of this sort of gallery is Martin Lawrence Galleries with locations in a dozen cities throughout the US.

I would add local galleries to this category-those small spaces that exist in most small cities and towns. Often, these galleries have very high-quality work and are well worth investigating.

With the "pyramid" analogy, there are of course many galleries that fit some where in-between.

Co-op galleries create opportunities for artists to show and obtain significant experience in the art world. Artists share the work and the expenses, and I highly recommend this avenue for many artists who live in areas that have this kind of gallery.

Vanity galleries are also an interesting way to enter the marketplace. Vanity simply means that you pay to show in the space and take on the costs of most of the event.

A friend, a talented young Virginia Artist, Anabele Ferguson, shared some of her experiences with me about her dealings with several situations in Washington DC.

The first was a rental (vanity) gallery. When she met with the owner (who had 17 years experience), he indicated that he required $2400 per year, with a 60% commission (to him) on all sales. In addition, he required that a catalog of the artist's work be printed at a cost to the artist of $16,000 for a run of 2,000, with 12 images of the artist's work and two critical reviews (Washington critics). For a smaller run with fewer images and only one critical review, the cost to the artist would be $12,000. An ample supply of the catalogs, of course, would be retained by the artist and provide handsome marketing tools for the future.

All of this looked very exciting to Anabela who is a prolific artist. The gallery owner, realizing that he would have access to several hundred paintings each year, immediately offered representation, then announced to the artist that he would take 15% of all her sales, *even those from other locations.*

Fortunately Anabela, who is an exceptional businesswoman with a framing and conservation business, saw the financial drawbacks of this kind of an arrangement. When she asked the gallery owner the volume of his sales per year (from his gallery) he refused to answer. She considered this to be a "red flag." In her view, if the gallery was, indeed, a profitable operation, the owner would be happy to share his success stories.

Upon reflection, Anabela realized some important things. What other artists this gallery represented (now and in the past)? Did these artists have a good sales record? Should she have contacted them? Fortunately, the artist did not pursue this arrangement, but she learned a great deal.

Her experience with a co-op gallery was instructive as well. She found a great space in Washington DC that appeared to be well run by a group of artists. She learned that each artist paid between $150-190 per month to be a part of the co-op and the privilege of having one or two rooms to hang his or her work *once every two years.*

With 21 members, the gallery had gross sales of $25,000 the previous year. Calculating quickly the profit to each artist, Anabela realized that this was a losing proposition for her.

Undaunted by her experiences, she continued to seek opportunities for showing in a legitimate gallery, as her goal was to get maximum exposure in a noteworthy area while building her client and mailing list.

She did find a gallery in the upscale Georgetown area of Washington DC where she had a better experience. This was a commercial gallery and frame shop in a prime retail area. The fee was $1500 for a six week period during the summer.

She coordinated her own public relations campaign, sending out good-looking press packets, initiated a massive email blast to her friends and collectors and provided the food and drinks for a modest, but well-choreographed, opening. The show yielded some sales, but as the artist says, "It could have been better, but the experience was worth it."

The Artist/Gallery Partnership

"Because of their interdependence," write Tad Crawford and Susan Mellon in their informative book, *The Artist-Gallery Partnership*, gallery and artist must depend on the integrity and high standards of professionalism of one another." Again, we artists must take the time to do the research necessary to enter into a business relationship with a gallery.

Concurrently, the gallery will want to know about the artist's training and background, other galleries representing the artist's work and the level of productivity that can be expected. Some artists create only a few works each year–others are highly prolific. The gallery will want to know if you are willing and able to accept commissions or special orders. Since the gallery stakes its reputation on honoring agreements with clients, the artist must be willing to work with budgets and deadlines.

Commissioned Work

If you are willing to accept commissions, you might consider developing a commission "policy" paper to add to your website and portfolio. Since the creation of an original work of art specific to a client's requirements takes a certain level of talent and expertise, I suggest that the process be outlined up-front.

Most often a commission arises out of a situation where a buyer or client has seen a particular work of art–either yours or another artist's. They will want certain modifications, such as the size or color palette. We artists must listen to the client and be prepared to ask questions.

It is helpful to have reference material available during the opening discussion. Sometimes this occurs online, so be prepared to receive and send images that can move the process along. I usually do some sketches from which the client may choose.

Once an image, size, color palette and price are agreed upon, the artist may request a 50% deposit on the work. In all my years of creating commissioned work, I have never had a problem. I usually send progress photos as the work is unfolding so that there are no surprises.

When the work is completed and shipped, the final payment is made. I always assure my clients that if they are not completely happy with their artwork, they may return it for a full refund. They must pay for the return shipping and insurance, of course. This takes the pressure off the client and I can always place the artwork in one of my galleries or modify it for a future project.

The truth is, once the clients have hung the work in their home or office, they fall in love with it!

Unsure about this? Then I would advise not putting yourself in this position. When you are ready to accept commissions you will know instinctively how to deal with the clients.

How to Approach Galleries

First, start locally and regionally. Put together a list of galleries and personally visit each gallery or dealer. Find out what they sell and see how closely it matches the art that you make.

At the same time, begin to immerse yourself in your local art community. The best way, by far, to get your art seen is to get to know people socially, through organizations or community activities, and to personally show your art at every opportunity. This may sound difficult and tedious, but it's what you have to do in order to get noticed and eventually establish yourself as a working artist.

In order to get a feeling of the gallery world, spend time perusing magazines, as well as the internet, to help you determine where your work may fit. This is the "homework" to which I am constantly referring.

Be sure to visit the Art Dealers Association of America online at http://www.artdealers.com for a listing of major galleries. There are many hundreds of galleries through-out the US that deserve reviewing as well. You might want to start in your state of region.

Many areas have Gallery Associations, such as the Santa Fe Gallery Association www.santafegalleries.net, or the Scottsdale Galleries www.scottsdalegalleries.com, for example. Just Google around and look at all the information that is at your fingertips.

It is becoming more common for galleries to post their portfolio review procedures on their websites. These should be followed. In many instances, they will accept an email online with your URL (website). They will know immediately whether your work will fit in with their gallery. This is why you need a smashing website!

If you are fortunate to get the attention of the gallery, you may be asked to send a hard copy of your portfolio, so be prepared for this.

As a former gallery owner, I appreciated artists who took the trouble to know about my gallery before approaching me. Often I spent considerable time reviewing portfolios and offering guidance to promising young artists. This is unusual, so if a gallery director or owner takes the time to give you guidance, be thankful.

In preparing for this book, I interviewed several successful gallery owners. There was a general consensus on how they preferred to be approached by artists.

They agreed that artists who are courteous and sensitive to the routines of the galleries were more apt to gain the attention of the owners and directors.

Most galleries have a "high" or busy season; therefore, it is best to approach them during the slow period or prior to the busy season when they are more apt to give your work the attention it deserves.

Those gallery personnel I interviewed indicated that they preferred to receive a hard copy of the artist's portfolio with a

CD included. (A return stamped envelope will guarantee its return.) They want to see high quality, printed images of the artwork along with a bio, artist's statement and pricelist. If an exhibition history and collector list were included that would be a bonus.

After sending a portfolio for review, you may follow up with a phone call within two or three weeks. Galleries are generally very busy, so it is wise to give them plenty of time to review your work.

Most galleries prefer that you ***not*** visit with a handful of slides. Rarely will you be well- received, and the slides held up to a light bulb or a window will ***not*** do justice to your work.

Directors generally screen portfolios for the Owner(s). It would be a good idea, then, to do your homework and know the name of the Director. (The *Art in America Annual Gallery Guide* lists the names of the directors.)

Alternative Spaces

In recent years, alternative spaces have increasingly assumed a higher profile with many of the screening practices of typical galleries. Artist's studios still remain a favorite of collectors, with low-rent storefronts and warehouses gaining acceptance.

Surely, there is nothing new in these ventures, but, in the current marketplace, the innovation in the face of limited opportunities is reaching full force.

Since many galleries prefer to take on artists who have a track record in showing and sales, these alternative spaces are great places for emerging artists to get visibility and establish an exhibition history. This practice has always been what I call a "chicken and egg" theory. It takes experience to have gallery shows, but where does one get the experience to be accepted into a gallery?

In every community there are opportunities, other than art galleries, in which to show artwork that may be of great benefit. I must emphasize the word "may" here. It may be worthwhile to check out car dealerships, bookstores, libraries, community centers, coffee shops, etc.

If you are considering alternative spaces, be sure that you understand the conditions or terms. What kind of commission will they take on each sale? Who will do the actual selling? Is there is insurance on the artwork?

In the late 1980s, I had an opportunity to show my work in a new, young high-tech corporation in downtown Washington DC. The lighting and wall space was spectacular and the number of people exposed to the artwork was relatively high. Large canvases were hung in the reception area, the conference rooms and in all of the executive offices.

One day, there was a fire that caused significant damage to the entire operation. If I remember correctly, it was a faulty coffee maker in the kitchen. Fortunately, there was insurance on the offices as well as the artwork! An appraiser was called in and a dollar amount was presented to me. I accepted the fee, and was (fortunately) able to clean and restore two of the paintings that had suffered smoke damage. Had this company been without insurance I would have lost a dozen very large paintings.

Again, I encourage you to do your homework. Know what kind of commitment you are making and what the benefits are. Draw up a consignment agreement for your protection and that of the exhibitor. (See Chapter 8 for information on Consignment Law.)

Some alternative spaces:

- Banks
- Civic Centers
- Churches & Synagogues

- Airports
- Furniture Showrooms & Design Centers
- Chambers of Commerce
- Public Offices
- Real Estate Offices
- Showcases of Homes (for sale)
- Model Homes
- Interior Design Firms
- Convention Centers
- Private Clubs (e.g., Golf Clubhouses)
- Inns & Spas
- Restaurants & Bars

The Big International Art Expos

During the last 40 years, art fairs, internationally, have become "the" place for seeing, selling and buying art on a large scale. These shows are a vital source for art lovers and collectors.

Each year the number of trade professionals, art collectors, artists, dealers, curators, critics and art enthusiasts from around the world increase.

These venues allow the participants to discover new developments in contemporary art as well as the experience of rare, museum-caliber artworks.

The "grandmother" of these art shows is Art Basel Miami Beach. This massive exhibition has become one of the most important art shows in the US, and a cultural and social highlight for the Americas, with 250 leading art galleries from North America, Latin America, Europe, Asia and Africa exhibiting.

This is a sister event to Switzerland's Art Basel, one of the most prestigious art shows, world wide.

The original New York Art Expo has grown into a huge operation, sponsoring events in Los Angeles and New York that generate millions of dollars in art sales.

Not only do these events feature exhibitions by top-quality art galleries, but they have exciting programs of special exhibitions, performance art, young galleries, and video art with parties and crossover events in music, film, architecture and design.

The West Coast Art & Framing Show attracts large numbers of people also. With more than 600 exhibitor booths, attendees get the year's first look at new products and images from a wide array of leading framing suppliers and art publishers. Attendees include retail frame shops, galleries, wholesalers, and production framing companies.

I attended this show in January 2008 in Las Vegas and had a very positive experience. The classes and workshops on business and framing were inspiring.

For artists wishing to find publishers for their work, these large shows are the best. Be sure to have quantities of great looking mini-portfolios, CDs, pockets full of business cards and very comfortable shoes!

While these well-financed, international art fairs attract top galleries, some are now offering spaces to independent artists. The fees for booths are high, but artists can share the fees and cut the expenses for maximum exposure to a world-class market.

You can visit these art fairs' websites and check out their offerings:

- www.artexpos.com
- www.torontoartexpo.com
- www.fineartexpo.com
- www.arizonafineartexpo.com
- www.artbaselmiamibeach.com
- www.art-miami.com
- www.sofaexpo.com

Smaller Local & Regional Art Fairs

Of course, there are the smaller art fairs in which we can all participate, if we like. Many of them are prestigious, juried operations that attract very skilled art makers. There are hundreds of these shows all across the country - some of them have been around for decades and attract millions of visitors/ buyers each year.

I keep up with these, and other juried shows, through a great resource - Juried Art Services.

www.juriedartservices.com. This is a free service where you can sign up to receive emails to alert you about upcoming deadlines for exhibitions and fairs. You can also log on and research all the upcoming exhibitions, read about their criteria and apply online. Their best function is the ability to upload your portfolio to their site from which you can draw upon when applying for various shows.

After you have uploaded and submitted all your images, you will see a preview of your artwork exactly as the jurors will see it. You can arrange the artwork on the screen in any order you choose by clicking on the position number you want each image placed.

When you select the art event for which you would like to apply, you simply select from your existing online portfolio those images that you wish to submit for that particular event. You can even pay the entry fee online.

Yes, this is a great service both to artists and jurors. Now get online and use it!

Another great opportunity for artists is **The Artful Home.** www.theartfulhome.com the leading source for artist-made home décor, gifts and jewelry shipped direct from artist's studios to customers' homes and businesses. Founded 24 years ago by Toni Sikes, it was known for years as The Guild. Based in Madison

WI, the operation has grown from a handful of artists to a major operation which attracts millions of trade professionals and collectors. This is the leading state-of-the-art internet operation for online art sales, world wide

Over the years, the criteria has become more rigorous, but those of us who are fortunate to be a part of The Artful Home have been given opportunities to show in their two major books: ***The Artful Home*** and ***The Sourcebook of Architectural & Interior Art.*** These two hardcover books are sent annually to more than 40,000 architects and interior designers who use them as ***the*** resource in their design projects.

For member artists, there is a long list of services including an artists' extranet where artists can manage their sales, plus commission opportunities are listed and marketing strategies are shared.

In addition, the monthly Artful Home catalog was sent to two million homes in 2008, and the website had 1.2 million visitors.

During 2009, two million visitors are expected. Special activities like studio sales are also coordinated by these creative people. Trade professionals have signed up to receive informational emails, which in 2009 are estimated to be seven million. This is serious business, therefore I urge those of you who are serious artists to submit your application now.

Submission guidelines for The Artful Home are on the juried art services website. www.juriedartservices.com

Another great online gallery resource is the Saatchi Gallery in London. Artists can sign on and upload their images, bio, collector's list and exhibition history for free! There is no commission to artists or buyers for work purchased through www.saatchi-gallery.co.uk

Let us not forget Art Magazines. ***Art News, Art in America*** and ***American Art Collector*** are at the top of my list. ***The American Art Collector*** is most valuable for collectors as they feature upcoming exhibitions, nationally, ***before*** they open. Paintings in advertisements are frequently sold before the shows are hung!

The Art in America Annual Guide to Galleries, Museums & Artists is a world-class resource for artists. Artists can have their own free listing, and there is an incredible list of galleries by state as well as a listing of national art consultants to whom you can send your portfolios.

Of course, there are scores of online galleries, magazines, directories and other valuable resources, but with space limitations, I am touching only on those that I highly recommend.

Keeping up with art news is essential in these challenging times. If you do not subscribe to ***Art Business News,*** now is the time! Best of all, it is free to artists. www.artbusinessnews.com I enjoy their webinars on such subjects as marketing and "going green."

Art World News is also free to the trade. Focused on making art publishers, galleries, artists, and framing shops and suppliers successful, they claim to be the best-read trade magazine serving the art and framing industry. You decide! www.artworldnews.com

"It's all a game of construction, some with a brush, some with a shovel, some choose a pen."

Jackson Pollack

"Have no fear of perfection, you'll never reach it."

Salvador Dali

"It's on the strength of observation and reflection that one finds a way. So wemust dig and delve unceasingly.

Claude Monet

CHAPTER 4

Agents, Art Consultants & Designers

Artists, these people--agents, art consultants and designers--are your greatest allies. Particularly in these challenging financial times, it is incumbent upon us to reach out to markets that are still pushing forward.

Sometimes agents are known as art reps (artist's representatives). Most own their own businesses and serve as the "go between" for artists and architects, galleries, interior designers, real estate developers, corporate buyers and even book publishers. Reps, agents and consultants differ from art dealers inasmuch as they do not buy and sell artwork as dealers do.

Art consultants work with collectors and corporate clients to help the client navigate the often complex work of building a fine art collection. Often, art reps have a broad and international network of contacts to bring appropriate material to the client's attention. They not only help clients make purchases, but also they can help clients sell works when the time comes to upgrade or to change the focus of the collection.

My agent, Sure Roderick, works exclusively in the west (NM, AZ, CA, NV, HA) and represents artists who are painters, furniture makers and even a fabulous kaleidoscope designer. She finds appropriate placements for her artists and takes a commission on sales. Some agents will accept a one-time placement fee. Most, however, ask for a 10% commission on sales. This, of course, must be factored into the artwork's price, as most galleries will take 50% of the artist's retail.

Having an agent takes much of the burden off working with a gallery or other outlet. He or she coordinates advertising, interviews, one-person shows, openings, etc. Agents also have a wider view of the art marketplace and can advise artists on where we should be showing, what galleries are opening (and closing) and future trends.

Art consultants and advisers appear in many forms. Some corporations hire art consultants to function like curators to organize and document their corporate art collection.

Collections such as the prestigious John Deere Collection in Moline IL are massive and carefully documented. The Deere administrative center was one of the last designs by the late Eero Saarinen. Situated on a 1,000-acre site overlooking two lakes, the design provided for showcasing an impressive international art collection.

Other art consultants work independently or in design consulting companies that implement projects in various markets such as hotels, cruise ships, resorts and residential projects. They search for unusual artwork in all forms.

Most galleries also provide art consulting services. Trained sales associates perform the function of art consulting by meeting with clients and working to provide and install artwork for homes and offices.

I maintain a list of art consultants to whom I send information on an annual basis. One firm received my information in 2000 and never responded until 2008 with a special request for artwork for a client in NJ.

Designers also create relationships with artists. A designer friend who excels in hospitality design works with a variety of artists and crafts people worldwide to provide exceptional treatments for her projects. I encourage you to approach designers in your area to establish rapport with them. Give them a portfolio of your work for their files.

These relationships are very important for artists, and they are worthy of your time to nurture them.

One of the most valuable resources for artists wishing to connect with art consultants is the **International Association of Professional Art Advisors,** 433 Third Street, Suite 3, Brooklyn, NY 11215. www.iapaa.org

In the mid-20th century, with the burgeoning presence of corporate America's skyscrapers, open-concept office space and corporate campuses, forward-thinking CEOs introduced art into these settings, creating the need for professional art management outside of the museum sector. In response to this need, the IAPAA was formed.

Goals were established which foster excellence in the art advisory field, maintain exemplary levels of professional practice, promote responsible art management, and advocate for the importance of the visual arts and their function in the private and public sector.

The membership of IAPAA is posted on their website.

The Art in America Annual Guide to Galleries is released every August and remains on the newsstands until they are sold out. Check your local book store or order online. This is a gold mine of valuable information. www.artinamericamagazine.com

The *Art Network* has lists for purchase that can be ordered online at artmarketing.com Their affordable and targeted mailing lists contain art world professionals such as corporate art consultants, interior designers, corporations collecting art, art publishers, licensing agents, reps, consultants and brokers, and more.

The U.S. Department of State has developed a program, **The Art in Embassies Program** to provide art to Embassies and State Department Offices throughout the world. Their online application process is very simple and provides great exposure for an artist.

Their goal is to promote the cultural identity of America's art and artists by borrowing original works of art by U.S. citizens for display in U.S. embassy residences worldwide. Each art exhibition is developed collaboratively between a United States ambassador and one of the State Department curators. They select both image-based and abstract work in all media.

What is the length of a loan?

The length of a loan is approximately two and one-half to three years, which coincides with the average length of an ambassador's tenure.

Who arranges and pays for shipping and insurance?

Art in Embassies hires professional fine art handlers to assemble, pack, crate and safely ship works of art to each embassy. The program insures each work during its transit to and from the embassy and while it is on exhibit at the residence.

Are lenders compensated in any way?

Lenders are not compensated financially. Their participation is documented in art exhibition publications and/or on the art website.

Submissions are reviewed on an ongoing basis. Artists may submit images in the following formats only:

- Artist Websites:
    1. Submit your URL
- jpg images:
    1. Submit no more than 10 images (total size of email not to exceed 1MB)
    2. Do not send multiple emails (include all attachments in one email)
    3. Include object information, and an artist's statement, resume or biography

Please do not expect an immediate response. Art in Embassies archives submissions for future consideration.

They do not accept unsolicited mailed submissions, as their incoming mail is irradiated. The process destroys slides, transparencies and disks.

The Hospitality Industry

A booming world-wide hospitality industry is acquiring artwork for a variety of settings. They obtain the artwork through architects, designers and design firms. If your work may meet the specific requirements of large commercial spaces, it would be wise to get your portfolio into the hands of the experts.

One of the finest design firms in the business is Hirsch Bedner Associates. You will enjoy their website: www.hbadesign.com

Graphic Encounter www.graphicencounter.com has provided professional fine art consulting services since 1970 to premier destination resorts and hotels worldwide. Graphic Encounter has partnered with distinguished interior designers, architects and purchasing agents to help them realize their vision for high-end hospitality and government projects worldwide.

Some of their clients include the Wynn Las Vegas, Caesar's Entertainment, Harrah's and other renowned resorts and casinos.

Another resource is Stacy "StacyO" Overgaard, an art consultant who provides artwork for the hospitality industry including murals and tapestries. Her website: www.artxpectations.com

"Do not fear making mistakes – there are none."

Miles Davis

"Nowadays people know the price of everything and the value of nothing."

Oscar Wilde

CHAPTER 5

Pricing & Licensing

Artists often have a difficult time pricing their work. When I asked several artist friends how they arrive at their prices, I heard many answers. The common theme was this: Pricing in the beginning establishes the pricing equations for the future. On other words, you cannot drop your prices, but you can increase them.

So, if you are at the beginning of your art career, look around and see with other artists of your level are charging for their work. Go into galleries and other art venues and do some comparison shopping. Make it a top-priority to research and read every article on pricing that you can find.

One marketing expert and artist, Jonathan Talbot has the most helpful guidance in his book, *The Artist's Marketing & Action Plan Workbook*. He goes into great detail on five ways to determine pricing, such as allowing career goals to determine price, allowing career accomplishments to determine price, competition and market prices, variable cost + average fixed cost + commission (if any) + profit = price.

As complicated as this is, there is validity to these methods.

Talbot asks the reader to list all the costs, fixed and otherwise, including studio rent, utilities, framing, paint, brushes, etc. This is a useful exercise for all of us to do on an annual basis. He goes on to walk the reader through a lengthy and helpful process.

Here are some of my suggestions to determine pricing. Look at artwork that is similar to yours in genre, medium and size to see what others are charging for their work. Review the artist's resume, awards and length of time showing and selling. Compare their career levels to your own.

Some artists make the mistake of pricing too low, which can be a big mistake. By establishing low prices the artist shows a lack of experience and lack of confidence. Art galleries sometimes encourage this, as they want to make a "quick buck," however, in the long term, it misrepresents the artist. Again, please do the necessary homework. Confer with artists whose opinion you respect. Consider all the costs of creating the artwork along with your time.

Once you have decided on a price, be sure to add in a sales commission if you are in galleries. The amount of profit is your decision. Make a pricelist that establishes the retail price. Do ***not*** put a wholesale price or artist's price. This gives the dealer latitude to charge whatever price they please, and takes control of the retail price away from you.

You will also want to have a consistent policy with regard to discounts. These are given as rewards for loyalty and patronage. Many galleries will want a 10% "cushion" which is split 50/50 between the artist and the gallery when a client purchases more than one of your works or is a repeat customer.

If the gallery wishes to discount more than the 10%, they should either contact you to establish an agreeable discount and split or they should absorb the discount above the standard 10%.

Be sure that your prices are consistent no matter where the artwork is shown. Some people make the mistake of charging less (retail) for work in smaller locales and more in large metropolitan areas. This makes no sense, as your effort, materials and other costs are the same. This is also insulting to collectors. Do we think we need to penalize collectors in the big cities and patronize those in small towns? An emphatic no.

Additionally, between the internet ***and*** showing and selling in several galleries, the prices must be consistent. Imagine how you would feel if you purchased a work of art and found out later that it was cheaper if purchased off some art website. The art world is really small, so being consistent is the answer.

Know where you are in your career path. Are you a beginning artist? An emerging artist, who has gained some recognition through awards and press? Have you been around for years – selling well? (If so, you should be writing this book!)

The cost of supplies, framing, shipping and advertising have increased substantially in the last few years; therefore, if you are still pricing your work the same as it was in 1998, wake up and increase those prices.

I must refer back to your greatest asset – your **name**. If you have received accolades for your work and have achieved some recognition in your area, your prices should be increased a little each year. Your sales determine your increases. If you have sold 3 pieces in the last year, don't raise them. If you have sold 75 pieces, yes – they should be increased.

More important is to confer with your gallery, if you have one. They will advise you on pricing, which should have some relevance to their entire stable of artists. Your work should not be priced higher than the best selling artist in the gallery.

My "home" gallery, Ventana Fine Art in Santa Fe, features the artwork by famous Native American artist John Nieto. The gallery has been representing him for decades and his colorful work just flies off the walls. My goal is to reach a fraction of Nieto's success. Everything is relative!

Studio Sales

This is an area that is rarely addressed and, therefore, very awkward. For artists fortunate to be represented by galleries, that relationship is primary. When clients reach out to the artist, they should be referred back to the galleries, as it is the galleries that have invested in promoting the work and should be the conduit through which sales are made.

In some cases where clients pre-existed the gallery relationship, these client/artist relationships should also be honored. Artists can offer up to a 25% discount for long-term collectors, but no more. The expectation that a 50% discount should be given is simply unfair and unrealistic.

These situations are fraught with anxiety, but it is time for artists to be open and businesslike. Standardizing the sales practices will minimize the angst for everyone concerned. In my experience, it is best to be open and above board in all business dealings. When questions arise, put them on the table and strive for an outcome where everyone wins.

Art licensing

This is an exciting area in the larger licensing market and can supplement an artist's income and increase exposure. Licensing is defined as leasing the right to use a legally protected name, graphic, painting, logo, saying or likeness in conjunction with a product, promotion, or services. It is usually accomplished by a formal agreement between the owner or agent of the mark (the Licensor) and the prospective Licensee, who is either a manufacturer, supplier of services, reproduction source, or an agent on behalf of them.

Licensing is an industry that now produces over $15 million worth of retail sales every hour, 12 hours a day 365 days a year. Little more than a decade ago, the licensing industry generated $4.9 billion worth of goods and services at retail. In 1982, the figure grew to $13.6 billion. This volume doubled only two years later to $26.7 billion and again by 1985, almost doubled to $50 billion! The 2003 LIMA Licensing Industry Survey estimates retail sales of licensed merchandise to be a $110 billion (based on royalty revenues of $5.831 billion) for North America alone. It is difficult to find another industry generating this rate of growth and sustaining it year after year.

Licensing is no longer simply the domain of a few specialized people. Nowadays, all major companies and the media consider licensing a significant marking tool. One could even say that it has become one of the most powerful contemporary forms of marketing and brand extension, and that it is being used in ever-increasingly sophisticated ways.

Artists often license their work for greeting cards, posters, book covers, internet graphics, clothing, or fabrics, and, of course, limited editions of the original work of art.

Licensing is usually based on a contractual agreement between two business entities: the owner or agent of the property, also known as the licensor and the renter of the rights, and the prospective licensee, in this case, the artist. The formal permission to use the owner's property is subject to certain terms and conditions, such as a specific purpose, a defined geographic area, and a finite time period. In exchange for granting the rights for a certain property to the licensee, the licensor obtains a financial remuneration. The basic component of this payment is the royalty, which is a percentage of the product sales involving your image.

A less attractive offer is the outright purchase of the image. In addition to a royalty agreement, a guaranteed minimum royalty, the guarantee, is usually required. The licensee has to pay this guarantee even in the face of total failure of the property. A percentage of this guarantee is normally paid as an advance.

Today there are overwhelming licensing opportunities that did not exist a little more than a decade ago. The availability of licensed merchandise has proliferated over the last decade, and corporate America has finally recognized the value of its brand names and unique products developed over decades. Now these invaluable, easily identified markets are licensed as a cost-effective means of brand extension and additional consumer awareness for the primary brand. It is the popularity and familiarity of these marks that help otherwise undistinguished products stand out from the crowd.

The artist will need to be comfortable with his or her image being used in this manner before entering into any such agreement. Art licensing can offer opportunities and benefits to both the artists as well as the manufacturers of the licensed goods.

The rationale for the artist to license a product is linked to increasing market exposure and image or name recognition at a consumer level without having to develop, produce, or market a new project. Furthermore, the artist as licensor receives legal protection, since licensing a "brand" or image for use in certain product categories prevents potential competitors from legally using that image to enter those categories. **In most cases the artist may retain the original work of art**, transferring only the right of reproduction.

The greatest economic advantage for the artist-licensor lies with the profits from royalty payments. Spoken in financial terms, an artist may receive from the licensee and average royalty payment of up to 5 percent of the wholesale price of each sold product. Due to the fact that there are no manufacturing or marking costs, these revenues translate directly to profits.

When you are ready to explore licensing opportunities, search the web and look for fine art publishing companies. There are several notable ones worth researching, such as Bentley Fine Art Publishing which has been around since 1977. www.bentleypublishinggroup.com

Two other highly successful ventures are Crown Thorn Publishing www.crownthornpublishing.com and Editions Limited. www.editionslimited.com

*"Picasso obviously viewed his art
as a business, which it was.
I view my business as an art,which it is.
You should view your work that way too."*

Donald Trump

"If you don't live it, you don't believe it."

Paul Harvey

CHAPTER 6

Record Keeping, Inventory & Taxes

Keeping records does not have to be painful. Since you have opened a separate checking account for your business, (do it now, if you haven't) your check receipts - with notations of what was purchased-will help enormously.

Online banking, of course, is the greatest thing since sliced bread. You can download your statements and file them away for tax preparation purposes. Of course, QuickBooks or another great accounting software program is the way to go. The new 2009 QuickBooks has a suite of services including the creation of a website, managing an inventory, invoicing-all the bells and whistles.

For most artists, setting up physical file folders for all their activities will do the trick: Income, studio expense, advertising, photography, art supplies, equipment, web and graphic design. Having a viable inventory tracking system is imperative, also.

Inventory System

A simple Excel file system will serve this purpose nicely. Most computers come with a Microsoft Office system installed which includes Excel. It is worth your time and effort to learn this program. It is not difficult, and it will actually save you a lot of time.

Create a simple spreadsheet that includes the title (alphabetically), size, medium, year created, location (use a code if your work is in several galleries or locations) and the retail price. This can be updated as new work is created and emailed to your galleries. You can also add other categories indicating whether the piece is on your website or whether it is framed, etc. The inventory should *work* for you. I use mine to track sales, commissions, payments, etc.

Set up your system, then update whenever necessary. You'll be happy you made the investment of time.

I know artists who have paintings scattered all over their studios, their homes and garages. One good friend and very talented artist has gorgeous paintings all over her house, studio, closets and garage. Often when she runs out of canvas she dives into the closets and paints **over** some really good work. When I visit her, I plead with her **not** to do this. In addition, she should be keeping accurate records of her inventory.

When Morris Louis, an astonishingly prolific artist died at age 49 in 1962, he left behind 650 resplendently beautiful canvases, of which all but 100 or so remained in his estate. Some 600 of the surviving paintings date from the nine-year period that constitutes his mature career.

Hundreds of rolled canvases were found in his basement. No inventory was kept. No photographs were taken. Can you imagine the consternation when his friend Clement Greenburg, famous art critic, and Mrs. Louis began unrolling canvases unable to determine the titles or the artist's wishes on how the paintings were to be displayed? To this day, there are arguments on "which end is up."

The lesson for all of us is to keep accurate records. Whether the artwork is stashed away in a storage bin or hanging above your fireplace, all of it should be documented.

Taxes

According to the IRS, a majority of visual artists are considered "self-employed" with regard to filing taxes. In a legal and taxpaying sense, this means that your "business" as an artist and you as an individual taxpayer are one and the same. There is no legal separation such as one would have in a corporation, partnership, LLC or other legal entity.

For the IRS, all deductible business expenses are those that are incurred in connection with your trade, business, or profession, must be "ordinary" and "necessary," must "not be lavish or extravagant under the circumstances."

The artist usually files a "Schedule C" as part of his or her regular 1040 income tax form, which is where you report your art income and expenses. The artist may file a form 8829 for the home office (studio) deduction and will also be required to pay self-employment tax (Schedule SE) on your net income (profit) as well as federal income tax.

All these forms are part of the year-end 1040 income tax filing. As a self-employed artist, you will usually be required to pay estimated quarterly taxes using Form 1040-ES if your Federal tax liability is over $1,000 for the year.

Equipment purchased is generally "depreciated" and written off over five to seven years on Form 4562. Depreciation is a technique for expensing or writing off purchases that have a useful life of greater than one year. In other words, a kiln or a printing press is intrinsically different in nature from a tube of paint, brushes, and clay or photo chemicals. Supplies such as inks, film, canvas, and welding materials will be written off or deducted in the year of purchase.

It does not take much analysis to see that these guidelines are not an exacting science. The artist has a large group of basic expenses that easily fit the above criteria: travel (hotel, meals, etc.), vehicle and transportation costs, equipment, art supplies, home studio expenses, legal and professional fees, gallery costs & commissions, etc.

If you convert your hobby into a legitimate business, you can deduct a net loss from other income you earn, such as wages and salaries. How does the IRS determine whether your activity is a hobby or a for-profit business?

IRS publications outline these nine criteria:

1. Whether you carry on the activity in a businesslike manner.
2. Whether the time and effort you put into the activity indicate you intend to make it profitable.
3. Whether you are depending on income from the activity for your livelihood.
4. Whether your losses from the activity are due to circumstances beyond your control (or are normal in the start-up phase of your type of business).
5. Whether you change your methods of operation in an attempt to improve the profitability.
6. Whether you have the knowledge needed to carry on the activity as a successful business.
7. Whether you were successful in making a profit in similar activities in the past.
8. Whether the activity makes a profit in some years, and how much profit it makes.

9. Whether you can expect to make a future profit from the appreciation of the assets used in the activity.

The primary determinant is your ability to make a profit at what you are doing. If your efforts result in a profit in three out of five consecutive years, your activity is presumed not to be a hobby by the IRS. If you don't meet the three-out-of-five rule, is all lost? Not necessarily, if you can prove to the IRS's satisfaction that you have made a genuine effort to earn a profit and that the reason you are not successful is related to special circumstances, the IRS might agree that your art is, in fact, a business.

This is often true for individuals engaged in the arts, where profits and successes are difficult to achieve. To increase your chance of gaining the IRS's recognition of your business, you must run your activity in a professional, businesslike manner. Having business cards and stationery printed, maintaining a separate business checking account and telephone number, keeping accurate records of the time you put in, and carefully documenting all business-related expenses helps establish you as a sincere business person.

The Internal Revenue Service places great credence on computerized accounting records as evidence of the artist's "businesslike" intent. Keep records of all exhibition entry fees (even including ones that you don't get into) and all gallery activity. In short, anything related to attempts to sell your artwork.

The visual artist is unique in the world of taxes. When you are looking for a tax preparer please make sure they have some experience in taxation for artists. Inquire about other tax-saving strategies for self-employed artists such as retirement plans, health insurance and the timing of deductions.

"It is better to be looked over than overlooked."

Mae West

"No masterpiece was ever created by a lazy artist."

Salvador Dali

Chapter 7

Marketing

I learned while working in the ad business many years ago that marketing and advertising are totally different.

Marketing is selling an idea; advertising is selling a product. A good example of marketing is the organization MADD (Mothers Against Drunk Driving), which has done an incredible job of creating an awareness of the perils of drunk driving. An advertising program is always connected to a product such as Coke, Nike, Cheerios, Dell Computers, etc.

In the case of artists, we need a dual approach: *marketing and advertising*. We need to promote our name and the idea that the work we create is of high quality and deserving of being seen, collected, shown and winning accolades!

Our advertising is specific--presenting our artwork or products to the public.

Most artists have trouble with the whole idea of marketing themselves, as they consider it to be superficial, self-centered, ego-maniacal or worse.

The truth is, no artist starts out well known!

Marketing can, and should, be done tastefully and with integrity. You want to attract attention, but the right kind of attention. As artists, we have the advantage of having a great "eye" so we can utilize our skills to create the image that best represents us.

Let the Media tell your Story

The mass media, newspapers, magazines, radio and TV can play a key role in your marketing plan. Because the actual printing, broadcast or distribution is free (to you), mass media can be the most cost effective way to promote your work.

News-based media, including daily newspapers and broadcast programs, are likely to give you coverage if you tell them about something that has recently happened or is about to happen: an exhibition, the unveiling of a new commission, an award or grant for an interesting project. You should approach magazines and weekly newspapers for feature articles.

Ask yourself, is my story newsworthy? Does it have mass appeal? Does the story span art and business? Maybe your new suite of paintings is not particularly newsworthy, but if they are hanging on the walls of a new restaurant in town that is about to open, *that* is a story. Be creative. Think about what art collectors read. How can you get your "product" before them without spending a fortune?

Your goal is to make it easy for reporters and editors to fill space in their publication or program. For example, send them great photos and invite them to a news-worthy event where they may film or photograph the unveiling of a new mural or the opening of a co-op gallery. Create an invitation list that may include local political or civic leaders.

Whether it is the ***Chicago Sun Times*** or the ***Plattsburgh Daily News***, your hometown newspaper is the most logical place to start. It is a good idea to work the media locally *and* regionally. Be sure that your press release and photographs meet the paper's style and standards. Similarly, local magazines, television and radio stations are all good media prospects, so long as you stress your local angle.

Go national if the story is big enough!

Before you contact the media, it is important to become familiar with the publications or programs. Do they cover the arts on a regular basis? Who is the arts editor? Do they use visual material? Can you submit your material online?

In some instances, you will submit your press release as an attachment to an introductory email. You will follow up with a hard copy of the press packet to the media contact.

You should send your press release two weeks before an event, with a follow up phone call after 3-4 days. Magazines work 3-4 months ahead, so plan accordingly.

Become a recognized expert. Whether it is quilt-making or etching, you can become known in your respective field, if you choose. Make yourself available to appear on local talk shows. You might discuss your business as an artist, your particular style or technique. Questions from callers or audience members can create an interesting format.

You might consider writing articles for trade publications such as ***Art Business News*** or the ***Artist's Magazine***, and give workshops at local colleges, universities and community centers.

As you achieve success in the mass media, capitalize on your coverage. Include copies of articles in your portfolio and email them to collectors. Media coverage adds to your resume and will be valuable for years to come.

Medial Contact List

Keep your media information in an easily accessible format such as an excel file or an old-fashioned rolodex. Include all the local and regional media contacts, including email addresses. This should be updated periodically.

Ask your colleagues and friends if they have contacts in the media. Do the homework. When you read an article in your local media that appeals to you, write a note to the author. Establish a network of media contacts through interaction and referrals.

Consider inviting the arts editor for a studio visit for a preview of your upcoming exhibit. Encourage your local gallery to have a special preview event for your collectors and the press. Remember that people always enjoy feeling special - capitalize on that!

Press Packet

Create a visually attractive packet that includes a well-written press release which outlines (in the first paragraph) who, what, when, and where. Be concise but include interesting details.

Include support material for your news or event such as a brochure, catalog, photocopy of award and captivating photographs. Put ***all*** the material on a CD as well.

This is where your name is emphasized in a powerful way. Your name should appear on the cover of the portfolio and on the letterhead, envelope and on the CD. A business card should be included that may be scanned into the writer or editor's contact file.

Catalogs

If we artists are fortunate, and work very hard, there comes a time in our career when the opportunity arises to have an exhibition–one which will advance our career and gain a high level of recognition.

At such time, it is wise to consider investing in a catalog that represents not only the works in the exhibition but serves to promote our career and our entire body of work. This validates a lifetime of hard work and artistic achievements. Do not pass this up!

Chances are, the gallery or museum will share the costs of such an endeavor and obtain the services of a professional art writer or critic to provide the introduction. In today's world, an exhibition catalog (whether it is a one-person or a group show) is an incredible asset and will help promote your career for many years.

Brochures

Brochures of an artists work were necessary prior to the Internet. Today, with the world-wide-web, and other more effective tools, a brochure is less important. Unless, of course you conduct classes or workshops–in that case you'll need brochures. Well-designed business cards with an image of your work, your website and contact information now serves the purpose of a brochure. This will drive people to your website, where your entire portfolio is beautifully showcased, along with any class schedule that you may have.

Websites

There is nothing more important in 2009 (and beyond) than having an artful presence on the Internet. A website is not just a digital version of your portfolio, it is much more.

It is important to work with a design professional or learn the skills yourself. As an artist you already have a good "eye," so perhaps you can translate some existing skills into new ones

Beyond showing high-quality images of your work, there should be an editorial side to the website which lists upcoming shows and events, articles and press (with downloadable pdf files), your bio and artist statement.

You might also consider a blog. I have avoided this with my website, as mine is heavy with content and a blog seems unnecessary. For some artists, the blog works beautifully. Be careful, as the collecting public may interpret a blog to be immature or silly since studies have shown that the majority of bloggers are between 13-17 years of age. Just be aware that perception means a lot in the art industry.

The electronic medium is very different from the print media and requires a different set of skills to produce an engaging "look." Visitors also have a very short attention span, so "hook" them with wonderful graphics and perhaps a music track. The goal is to be added to their list of "favorite" websites which they visit often.

Your site may require substantial maintenance, but it will attract loyal visitors, collectors, students, and fellow artists to your site.

If you are exploring the possibility of having a website, there are many options for websites that are free or very affordable.

www.Artcloud.com - A great website where artists can upload artwork, statement and more.

www.weebox.com - Flash-based website creator with a drag-and-drop interface. You do have to host through them. A good example: www.emiliorobba.com

www.SiteKreator.com - You can instantly design, build and host a fully-branded website for personal or business use. This is an artist's website that is beautifully designed: www.jaynerose.com

www.Leafletter.com - Allows you to create a "little web site" that you can then distribute anywhere (social networks, blogs, other websites).

www.SynthaSite.com - Browser-based website creation tool that allows you to collaborate with friends or colleagues. Also has lots of widgets, templates and other useful components.

www.Weebly.com - With Weebly, you can create a fully branded website using a drag and drop interface, and change your design any time.

www.CreataPlace.com - Create a professional portfolio website without programming. Very affordable.

www.BuiltSmarter.com - Tons of templates available, depending on the price you're willing to pay, built-in modules and customization also available.

www.sampa.com - Free website and hosting. There is an ad bar that runs across the top of your. This is mostly for sharing family photos and blogging.

www.allwebcodesign.com - Royalty free music. Nice MP3 sound for websites, very inexpensive.

www.allwebcodesign.com - Worth investigating.

www.artistsregistry.com - provides several levels of membership one of which includes a $100 one-page website with three images and an artist's statement. A listing will include your name in bold, with a link to your portfolio, your address, phone number, style of work, link to your website and email, and photo links of your work placed throughout the Website. Certainly worth investigating.

My personal favorite is www.askart.com

Ask Art has an average of 70,000 visitors per day. You can set up an artists "studio" in just a few minutes. If you choose to sell your work on that website, there is no fee, so you receive the payment directly. The cost is only $16.50 per month. The best feature is the ability to update your material whenever, and however, you wish.

When you are ready for a high-quality, professional website, do your homework and create something that represents you and your work. There are templates available online that you can purchase. Be sure to ask for a trial, so that you can study the software to determine its flexibility, accuracy (especially color) and its marketability.

Go online and review other artist's presentations. You will notice that there are two types of websites. One is html (hyper-text markup language) which is simple and easy; consisting of scroll-down pages and thumbnails of images. These images, when clicked on are enlarged. Look at the clarity of the images. How large are they? Do they represent the artist in a positive, artful way way?

The newer "flash" sites, while more costly are animated and interactive. Usually the images are much sharper and consistent with the actual artwork.

The goal is to have an easily-navigated, image-driven website that shows the artwork in a large format, as people hate to open thumbnails. Seriously! Look for formats that allow for easy maintenance on your part or your webmaster or webmistress. Avoid a website that scrolls down forever. This is amateurish, at best.

Remember to copyright your website also. When a viewer "right-clicks" on your images they should see the words: ***copyrighted material***, and therefore not downloadable. This is very important. You don't want people to download and copy your work. Images are always low resolution making it difficult to enlarge beyond screen size.

Consider, also, selling items on your website. Your instructional video, a catalog from an exhibition, a book, or limited editions can create wonderful passive income for you. Paypal is an online purchasing service that charges a minimal fee for each transaction.

Once the website has been completed, it must then be marketed on the web. At a minimum, the site must be recognized by the major search engines. Your web person should be able to do this for you. It is called search engine optimization (SEO).

To market your website, you can pay a certified SEO person, or you can do it yourself. To be seen by the search engines, you insert a set of metatags or keywords for the search engines to see.

An example of this: If you are a California artist specializing in paintings of Yosemite in pastel and watercolor, and you conduct classes, you might insert the following: Your name, California landscape artist, Yosemite paintings, colorful florals, pastels and watercolors, classes for beginners through advanced students. This way if someone types in the search bar, "Yosemite paintings," your website should show up. This takes a fair amount of experience, so having a professional prepare your website for submission may be the way to go.

You need only to submit your website to the major search engines **once!** Often the search engines give you a set of "code" that is implanted into your website.

Submitting your website multiple times has no effect on your position in the search engines, nor does it affect the frequency with which the search engines will visit your website. This may not be true of the minor search engines, but for the crawlers that power the major search engines discussed below, you only need to submit ***one*** time.

What are the major Search Engines and Directories? **The top 5 search engines comprise more than 95% of all traffic** your website will receive from search engines. Below is a comprehensive list of the major players in the search engine scene.

Major Search Engines

Google (http://www.google.com). Often called the greatest search engine on the Internet, it is also the most popular according to recent Nielson/NetRatings polls. This search engine is entirely free for the primary listings and offers paid listings at the top of the search results, as well as their Ad Words program which shows small text banners on the right hand side of the search results.

Google bases its search results on website content as well as their patented PageRank algorithm which factors in links from other websites to determining your rank in the search results. Submit to this website at http://www.google.com/addurl.html and your website should be in the index within a month, sometimes two.

Yahoo (http://www.yahoo.com). Second most popular and probably the most famous of all search engines, this icon among web portals controls the search results on MSN.com, AltaVista.com and Alltheweb.com, in addition to its own search results. Submission is free, and I wouldn't recommend paying for inclusion in this directory at this time, though paying to be in the directory is a good idea if you can afford the $300/year. To submit your website to the search engine go here: http://submit.search.yahoo.com/free/request

MSN.com (http://www.msn.com). The third most popular search engine, MSN, does not currently provide its own search results. The results found on MSN are actually provided by Yahoo, and you can be listed in MSN by submitting through Yahoo at the link above. MSN does plan to offer their own search results in the future, and I believe that they are using the old Inktomi index as their starting point, so you might want to submit here: http://free.submit-it.com/msnsubmit.htm

AOL (http://www.aol.com). This popular search engine uses Google search results as its primary and paid listings. See Google.

AllTheWeb (http://www.alltheweb.com). Purchased by Yahoo, this once-promising search engine now uses Yahoo results and will probably be used as a side project by Yahoo for various purposes.

AltaVista (http://www.altavista.com). One of the oldest search engines on the Internet, AltaVista was showing its age until Yahoo purchased it in 2004. It now uses Yahoo results and is basically just another portal for Yahoo.

AskJeeves / Teoma.com (http://www.ask.com and http://www.Teoma.com). The Teoma index powers both the popular Ask.com website and its sister site, Teoma.com. You can only get into this index through being found by the Teoma Crawler, or via paid Inclusion which you can order through http://www.positiontech.com/askjeeves/index.htm

The above are the main search engines on the web where you can submit your website. If you know a website that is not on the above list, chances are it is using search results from one of the above search engines or indexes.

Slide Registries & Competitions

There was a time, prior to the internet, when slide registries were a good form of marketing. Now with the Internet, those in search of art for a variety of reasons rely solely on the internet. I encourage you submit your work to registries via the Internet.

www.artistsregistry.com (for example) is an International community of Visual and Performing Artists. They connect artists together with galleries, museums and arts organizations as well as placing your artwork before the eyes of thousands of art collectors worldwide.

Put your time and effort into compiling a wonderful portfolio of images specifically formatted for the web.

Evelyn Daniel-Putnam, President of Daniel Fine Art Services in Laguna Beach, California whose company finds artists from all over the world via the World Wide Web says, "It's all Internet. It used to be slide registry. Now it's the web to' look' at the artist's website."

Her company is a preeminent art-consulting firm for luxury hotel and casinos, managing projects worldwide for clients such as Hilton, Ritz-Carlton and Hyatt.

http://artdeadline.com established in 1994, this is an outstanding online program that has a $24 annual membership fee. For this nominal fee you can take advantage of the following:

Juried Exhibits
Call for Entries
Art Competitions
Artist Grants
Jobs for Artists
Public Art RFP's
Percent-for-Arts
Purchase Calls
Internships
Art Festivals
Financial Aid
Scholarships
Residencies
Fellowships
Commissions
Portfolio Reviews
Proposal Calls
Publication Calls

This is an example of one of their listings:

International Deadline: March 31, 2009 - This competition is for Direct Art Magazine, Volume 16, Fall 2009 edition. The competition is for twenty six publication awards. Artist winners of the competition will, at no cost to the artist, have their work appear Volume 16 of the Direct Art Magazine.

The competition is open to all artists, national and international, working in all media. All forms of painting, drawing, sculpture, photography, graphics, mixed media, digital and installation art are eligible. Entrants must be 18 years of age or older to apply. Complete submission guidelines are on the website.

Galleries seeking artwork also post their submission guidelines. An example is the following:

Inaugural Exhibition: Still Point I

National Deadline: March 16, 2009 - Still Point Art Gallery (in Maine) invites submissions from emerging and established artists for its inaugural exhibition: Still Point I. Three Artists of Distinction

> will be chosen who will be invited to participate in a group show in the spring of 2010...

Artists may also submit and manage their artwork online. No more slides or cumbersome paperwork! Starting at $9.95 artists can show and sell their artwork on http://www.artdeadline.com

*"Did you ever observe to whom the accidents happen?
Chance favors the prepared mind."*

Louis Pasteur

*"Life shrinks or expands in proportion
to one's courage."*

Anaïs Nin

CHAPTER 8

Consignment Law & Copyright

Never has it been so important to understand your rights and responsibilities as an artist. Who is responsible when artwork is damaged? What do you do when a gallery goes belly up?

In the current economic climate, many galleries are unable to pay their bills. If you are represented by one of these "imperiled" galleries, what happens if a creditor comes in and takes the inventory in lieu of payment?

Do you have rights? Do you have a consignment agreement? Does your agreement protect you and your artwork in such an instance?

Consignment sales come with plenty of risks. Consider the artists left holding the bag when a Minneapolis gallery filed for bankruptcy owing artists $97,000. One of the artists said, "We're the canaries down the coal mine. When the gas comes we're the first to die."

So what's an artist to do?

There are three types of legal protection for consignors: the Uniform Commercial Code, state consignment law, and written consignment agreements. You may, however, find some of the laws difficult to comprehend, inconsistent and expensive to enforce.

The Uniform Commercial Code

Every state has adopted a version of the Uniform Commercial Code (UCC), a set of uniform business laws that protect consignments. For instance, under the UCC, if damage to your artwork results from the gallery's negligence, the gallery must pay for the loss. If the damage is not the fault of the gallery--for example, there's flooding or a fire--the gallery may, or may not, be liable, depending on how the courts in that state interpret the UCC.

The UCC is not always so helpful, however. Under the UCC, if a gallery files for bankruptcy, the gallery's creditors can seize your consigned goods as payment for the gallery's debts!

In other words, anyone owed money by the gallery can take your artwork as payment. You must stand in line behind the other creditors in bankruptcy court and hope that the judge awards you some compensation for your consigned goods.

You can avoid this unhappy outcome by fulfilling one of following three requirements under the UCC:

File a UCC-1 form (known as UCC Form 1) at the time of the consignment in the county where gallery is located.

Have the gallery owner post a sign telling the public that the goods are consigned (this option is not available in all states).

Prove that creditors were aware that the gallery sold consigned goods.

Although artists rarely use these cumbersome UCC requirements, you may find it worthwhile--in the case of high-ticket, one-of-a-kind work of art--to file the UCC form. The filing creates a lien (a legal claim over property), elevating you to the level of a "secured creditor" and putting you at the head of the line in bankruptcy court. If you do file the form and obtain the lien, you must remove the lien at the time of any sale.

Having the store or gallery post a sign--the second UCC requirement--may seem like an awkward request, but more and more stores and galleries are complying with such requests. Include a requirement in your consignment agreement that the gallery post a notice such as "Artwork at this gallery is sold under the terms of consignment agreements." As noted above, this may not be effective in all states.

Most artists will find the third requirement difficult to accomplish since it requires proof that creditors of the gallery were aware of the consignment. Some consignors (the artists or crafts workers) have accomplished this requirement by sending the creditors a copy of the consignment agreement. As you can imagine, the average artist who does not know who the creditors are and who may not have a written consignment agreement would find this impractical.

State Consignment Laws

Because the UCC has proven to be frightening for artists and crafts people, many states have passed special consignment laws to protect artists from gallery abuses and bankruptcy. So far, 31 states have passed art consignment laws--Alaska, Arizona, Arkansas, California, Colorado, Connecticut, Florida, Georgia, Hawaii, Idaho, Illinois, Iowa, Kentucky, Maryland, Massachusetts, Michigan, Minnesota, Missouri, Montana, New Hampshire, New Jersey, New Mexico, New York, North Carolina, Ohio, Oregon, Pennsylvania, Tennessee, Texas, Washington and Wisconsin.

Most of these state laws provide a shield from a consignee's bankruptcy by eliminating the ability of creditors to seize consigned goods. (In reality, enforcing these laws usually requires hiring a lawyer and filing claims in bankruptcy court.) Half of the state laws require a written consignment agreement as a condition for enforcing the law.

Determining whether your artwork qualifies as 'art' under state laws can be confusing. Many state consignment laws apply only to 'fine art.' Fine art is traditionally defined as a painting, sculpture, drawing of graphic art, or print, but not multiples. Other states--for example, Arizona and Ohio--specifically include crafts under consignment laws (defining them as any work made from clay, textile, fiber, wood, metal, plastic, or glass).

Consignment Agreements

Traditionally, most artists have used oral agreements to establish consignments. Today, you should really use a written consignment contract, since clarifies the relationship between you and your gallery and, most importantly, it is required under many states' consignment laws.

Your consignment agreement should include:

- The store or gallery's responsibility for insuring your property.
- The commission (%) paid to the artist.
- How soon after the sale(s) will the artist be paid? Usually 30 days.
- A complete inventory list of items consigned, including title, size and retail price.
- List any special considerations such as shared costs of advertising.

Also, if possible, include an attorney fee provision (the loser in a lawsuit pays the winner's attorney fees) and an arbitration provision (requiring settlement by a private arbitrator, not a judge). These provisions create incentives for rapid settlement of all (non-bankruptcy-related) disputes.

A written agreement provides practical benefits, but using common sense and your business radar provides the best protection. Ask other artists about their experiences in particular galleries before committing to a relationship. There are galleries that have a terrible track record on paying artists.

One of my galleries in Beverly Hills closed a few years ago and ran off with all the artwork. I had only a verbal agreement with them, so I was burned badly. Don't let this happen to you!

In the case of a gallery not paying its creditors, this, or similar wording should be included in your consignment contracts:

> *"Title to and a security interest in any works consigned or proceeds of sale under this Agreement are reserved to the Artist. In the event of any default by the Gallery, the Artist shall have all the rights of a secured party under the Uniform commercial Code (UCC) and the works shall not be subject to claims by the Gallery's creditors."*

In addition, risk of loss/damage must be covered:

> *"All risk of loss or damage of the artwork will pass to the Consignee when the Products are in the Consignee's physical possession. The Consignee shall insure the artwork against all risks against which such goods are customarily insured, including insurance for theft and damage, and shall provide evidence of such insurance coverage to the Consignor as and when requested. If the artwork are damaged or lost while in the Consignee's physical possession, a Sale of artwork will be deemed to have occurred and the Consignee will reimburse the Consignor in the amount of the damaged or lost*

artworks' respective Retail Prices, less the Consignee's Commission."

Copyright and reproduction should also be covered in artist's agreement with a paragraph such as this:

"The artwork may not be photographed, sketched, painted, or reproduced in any manner whatsoever without the express, written consent of the Artist."

When there are editions or a publisher is involved, the artist must have the right to control the use of the plates, the numbers in each edition, etc.

To emphasize again, the artist must be aware of consignment laws pertaining to the states in which his or her work is represented.

Requiring art dealers, exhibition sponsors, galleries and other sales entities to use contracts is not a sign of mistrust, but rather an indication that you are serious as an artist/business person. You are demonstrating good faith in establishing a good working relationship by outlining ahead of time any issues that may come up in the future, avoiding conflicts and heartburn for all parties.

https://www.legalzoom.com Legal Zoom is a great online resource. I have been using it for years for wills and other legal forms. You can, for $14.95, download a consignment form which can be used for agreements with many galleries. You will need to **insert the paragraph (opposite) regarding creditors' claims** to artwork for your protection in case your gallery is not paying its bills.

Copyright

Copyrighting your creative work protects it from unauthorized use. With a registered copyright, you control how your work is reproduced, distributed and presented publicly.

The 1978 Copyright Act has made copyright procedures very simple. It reads: "Any artwork is protected by copyright as soon as it comes into being as long as an artist places a copyright notice on the work. This consists of "Copyright," "Copr.," or "©," the artist's name (or abbreviation by which the name can be recognized or an alternative designation by which the artist is known), and the year of creation. The copyright lasts for the duration of the artist's life plus fifty years.

Artists working in every medium may copyright their work. This includes: painting, photography, sculpture, drawing, graphics, multimedia, models, diagrams, film, tapes, slides, records, DVDs and compositions.

With the Internet, copyright registration forms may be downloaded from the Copyright Office Website. There are different forms for different types of works -- for example, form TX is for literary works while form VA is for a visual art work.

http://lcweb.loc.gov/copyright/forms

If you plan to manufacture or license your artwork, you will need to obtain a design patent. You can do this online also at:

http://www.uspto.gov/Web/menu/tm.html

Or, by phone:
U.S Copyright Office: information 202-707-3000
U.S Copyright Office Forms: 202-707-9100

Non-Government Websites

Artists Rights Society: www.arsny.com

ASMP Copyright Application Tutorial: http://asmp.org/commerce/legal

University of MI Extensive Resource Links: http://www.lib.umich.edu/copyright

Copyright Website: http://www.benedict.com

Stanford University Libraries: http://fairuse.stanford.edu

10 Myths About Copyright Explained by Brad Thompson: http://www.templetons.com/brad/copymyths.html

Do countries outside the U.S. offer the same copyright protection?

Copyright protection rules are fairly similar worldwide, due to several international copyright treaties, the most important of which is the Berne Convention. Under this treaty, all member countries--and there are more than 100, including virtually all industrialized nations--must afford copyright protection to artists who are nationals of any member country.

All countries in the Berne Convention must offer copyright protection that lasts for at least the life of the author plus 50 years and must be automatic without the need for the author to take any legal steps to preserve the copyright.

In addition to the Berne Convention, the GATT (General Agreement on Tariffs and Trade) treaty contains a number of provisions that affect copyright protection in signatory countries.

Together, the Berne Copyright Convention and the GATT treaty allow U.S. artists to enforce their copyrights in most industrialized nations and allow the nationals of those nations to enforce their copyrights in the United States.

How are copyrights enforced?

If someone violates the rights of a copyright owner, the owner is entitled to file a lawsuit in federal court. The owner of the copyright will have to provide ample proof that the laws were infringed upon.

Trademarks

A trademark is a distinctive word, phrase, logo, domain name, graphic symbol, slogan or other device that is used to identify the source of a product and to distinguish a manufacturer's or merchant's products from others. Some examples are Nike for sports apparel, Gatorade for beverages, and Microsoft for software.

Consumers often make their purchasing choices on the basis of recognizable trademarks (sometimes referred to simply as "marks"). For this reason, the main thrust of trademark law is to make sure that trademarks don't overlap in a manner that causes customers to become confused about the source of a product.

If two similar trademarks are being used by companies that provide different products or services, there may not be a trademark conflict. This is especially true if the two businesses serve only local markets and are hundreds of miles apart.

However, in the case of trademarks that have become famous--for example, McDonald's--the courts are willing to grant much broader protection and prohibit almost all use of the trademark (or anything close to it) by anyone other than the famous mark's owner.

For instance, McDonald's was able to prevent the use of the mark McSleep by a motel chain because McSleep traded on the McDonald's reputation for a particular type of service (quick, inexpensive, standardized). This type of sweeping protection is authorized by federal and state statutes (referred to as anti-dilution laws) designed to prevent the weakening of a famous mark's reputation for quality.

In order to be eligible for trademark protection, a word or phrase must be "distinctive"--unique enough to help customers recognize a particular product in the marketplace--rather than generic, like "The Coffee House." A mark may either be inherently distinctive (the mark is unusual in and of itself, such as Diesel fashions) or may become distinctive over time because customers come to associate the mark with the product or service (for example, McDonald's restaurants).

What is a service mark?

For practical purposes, a service mark does the same thing as a trademark--but while trademarks promote products, service marks promote services and events. Some familiar service marks are: Amazon.com (retail website), Jack in the Box (fast food service), Kinko's (photocopying service), Blockbuster (video rental service), CBS's stylized eye in a circle (television network service), and the FedEx logo (delivery services).

What is trade dress?

In addition to a label, logo, or other identifying symbol, a product may come to be known by its distinctive packaging--for example, the yellow packaging of Kodak film. Similarly, a service may become known by its distinctive decor or shape--for example, the orange-like structure of Orange Julius juice stands.

Collectively, these types of identifying features are commonly termed "trade dress." Because trade dress often serves the same function as a trademark or service mark--the identification of goods and services in the marketplace--trade dress can be protected under the federal trademark laws and in some cases registered as a trademark or service mark with the U.S. Patent and Trademark Office (USPTO).

What is a collective mark?

A collective mark is a symbol, label, word, phrase, or other mark used by members of a group or organization to identify goods, members, products, or services they render. Collective marks are often used to show membership in a union, association, or other organization--for example, ILGWU is a collective mark for the members of International Ladies Garment Workers Union.

A collective mark can also be used as a trademark or service mark. For example, when the Girl Scouts sell cookies with their collective mark on the package, that indicates that goods are a product of the organization (that is, they are Girl Scout brand cookies). This way, the same collective mark can be used to indicate membership or to sell products and services.

What is a certification mark?

A certification mark is a symbol, name or device used by an organization to vouch for products and services provided by others--for example, the "Good Housekeeping Seal of Approval." This type of mark may cover characteristics such as regional origin, method of manufacture, product quality and service accuracy.

Some examples of certification marks are: UL (the Underwriters Laboratories certification of electrical standards), Stilton cheese (a product from the Stilton locale in England), and Harris Tweeds (a special weave from a specific area in Scotland).

What, you may ask, does this have to do with my art business? Some artists have a trademark that sets them apart in the marketplace. For example, an artist/friend uses the phrase "Brush Strokes" to advertise her work, her services, her website and her classes.

If another artist were to use this phrase, there could be a problem. My advice (as always) is to do the homework. If you are considering a phrase like "Layering Light" (my trademark for DVDs, classes, etc.) you will get into trouble.

We need to be aware of this to avoid serious problems for our art businesses!

"Shall I tell you what I think are the two qualities of a work of art? First, it must be indescribable and second, it must be inimitable."

Pierre Auguste Renoir

"All true artists, whether or not they know it, create from a place of no-mind, from inner stillness."

Eckhart Tolle

CHAPTER 9

A Winning Portfolio

What can be more important for an artist than a dazzling portfolio? Put yourself in the viewer's shoes. What would make them pick up the phone and call you to say, "I want you?"

To become successful in today's art market, you must not only master the technical skills required in your art medium, understand of the business of art, but also prepare a portfolio that represents you clearly and consistently.

Remember, no matter what you've heard or read, your work doesn't stand alone. Whenever a gallery owner, museum curator or art consultant reviews your portfolio, the memory of your work will be only part of what you leave behind.

When presenting a portfolio, not only the artist's work is being judged, the *artist* is also being judged. Is this artist serious? Will he or she succeed in the art world? Are they worthy of being represented?

Just as packaging plays an increasingly important role in product marketing, you are as integral to your presentation as your images. A successful portfolio presentation is absolutely necessary if you expect to become represented by a gallery or make a lot of sales.

When a gallery chooses to represent you, they make a huge investment of time and energy. They also invest in you through advertising, mailings etc. Falling in love with your work is the beginning of a great relationship and is a positive predictor of good sales.

Your artist portfolio should impress viewers with your vision and with how well you have mastered the technical aspects of your work. To go along with your portfolio, you should provide good artist support materials.

Portfolio Design

A simple three-ring binder with clear sheet protectors is perfectly adequate. Be sure to avoid the sleeves that are non-glare as they will distort the images.

There is no need to invest in a fancy leather portfolio. Keep it simple and clean. Most art supply stores have a variety of portfolios to choose from. Those with zippers work nicely and will keep the material clean.

A good portfolio should have continuity and provide viewers with an organized view by subjects or styles.

I cannot stress enough the need for printing the images correctly. There is nothing worse than looking at a portfolio and having the artist say, "The images are a little dark." Use a professional photographer and commercial printing service if necessary. In the long run, you'll be happy you did.

The sizes of the images should be consistent and centered on a letter-size page (or larger) which includes the title, size and medium below the image. If you work in several mediums, group them (i.e. pastels, watercolors, etc).

Of course, if you are a designer or a photographer, you may want to use larger-sized portfolios.

It is best to present only one thematically unified body of work. Do not confuse the viewer with unrelated images. For example if your best work is landscapes, don't throw in portraits. Show your strongest work first and trust that your success will allow you to present additional work in the future.

Limit the number of works to no more than 20. The main objective is to introduce your work to the gallery. You do not need to include everything you have created in the last 10 years! Make the experience of looking at your work as pleasant and positive as possible.

Since it is often difficult to be objective about your own artwork, you might ask your mentor, teacher or another artist whom you respect to view and critique your portfolio prior to showing it to a gallery.

I do not advise you to send slides in your portfolio. You can be sure that most gallerists do not have the time or inclination to put the slides into a carousel and view them on a proper screen in a dark room. They will simply hold the slides up to a light bulb or window. This does a great disservice to you and your work.

That is not to say that for some competitions slides are required. That is a whole other story.

Support Materials

In addition to the artwork, your portfolio should include a biography, an artist statement, collector list, exhibition history and pricelist. If your exhibition history and collector list is thin, include these in your biography. Awards and accolades should be included in your biography also. Try to keep each of these items to one page. You may include press clippings, but be sure they are properly presented in sleeves.

Put everything on a CD as some galleries will keep that on file and return the hard copy of your portfolio to you.

Bio and Statement

Remember they are different. The bio is a resume and primarily a list of things - education, exhibitions, awards, etc. The statement is a short narrative about you and your work in which you can describe your painting style, your approach or your philosophy, if you wish.

How long should the artist statement be?

It is better to make your artist's statement too short than too long–most people simply won't have the patience to read a lengthy treatise and many will be put off before they've even started. Aim at around 100 words or three short paragraphs.

There are many resources to help you write your bio and statement. The Artists Foundation in Boston has a few good samples on their website: www.artistsfoundation.org

Packaging

Your work should be presented in an appropriate portfolio case or shipping case. Cases are usually available from good local photography or art supply stores. You can also purchase them through mail order companies. I have a beautiful aluminum portfolio that showcases my work on metal. It is a real eye-catcher and has served me well.

When shipping your portfolio to a gallery, be sure to include a self-addressed, stamped envelope if you wish to have it returned. Of course, if you are presenting your work to a local gallery, it will not need a shipping envelope.

Check out some of the wonderful envelope designs at your art supply or office supply store. You may want to create custom-designed shipping labels for this purpose.

Follow Up

Keep a simple list of galleries, curators and art consultants whom you have contacted. Include the following information: name of reviewer, name and address of the gallery, telephone number, date of review, type of work presented, impressions, comments, what material you left behind, results of the review and type of follow-up you have planned.

Be sure to send a thank-you card to the person who looked at your portfolio. Send a postcard of one of your images, so that it will remind the reviewer of what work you presented.

You can create and send real snail mail postcards with Hazel Mail for $1.50. http://www.hazelmail.com The quality is excellent and you can upload your own images, write a message, and they will send to the destination of your choice.

"I believe that if it were left to the artists to choose their own labels, most would choose none."

Ben Shahn

"Being good in business is the most fascinating kind of art. Making money is art an creating good business is the best art."

Andy Warhol

"I am a deeply superficial person."

Andy Warhol

Chapter 10

Consider "Multiples"

Today's sophisticated digital printing processes make it possible for artists to create high-quality editions both limited and open for generating sales and exposure.

Editions are perfect for the new, young collector who will eventually be in a position to purchase your originals. You can also put your editions on your website for sale.

Giclées are the most popular form of creating multiple images. The earliest prints were created in the early 1990's on the Iris Graphics models' continuous inkjet printers (the company was later taken over by Scitex, now owned by HP). Iris printers were originally developed to produce prepress proofs from digital files for jobs where color matching was critical such as product containers and magazine publication.

Their output was used to check what the colors would look like before mass production began. Much experimentation took place to adapt the original Iris printer to the production of color-faithful, aesthetically-pleasing reproductions of artwork. Early prints were relatively fugitive and tended to show color degradation after only a few years.

Now, the use of high-tech archival inks and printing substrates has extended the longevity and light-fastness of these prints.

There are many competent "print on demand" type giclée printing companies that may be found online. Artists can upload their images, the prints can be completed and "drop" shipped to clients, worldwide. No longer is it necessary to print a large quantity of prints to be stored away until they are sold.

You can shop around, get pricing online and ask for samples of papers that they use. Ask other artists who have giclées for sale to recommend a printer to you.

You might look into other printing options including monotypes, lithographs, woodblock prints, and serigraphs. If there are galleries showing and selling your originals, you should coordinate with them. They may have concerns about showing both original work and multiples, so you might consider creating an entirely new look for your multiples which would not "compete" with your original work.

"Being a good artist is the toughest job you could pick,
and you have to be a little nuts to take it on
I love them all."

Charles Saatchi
Saatchi Gallery, London

CHAPTER 11

Networking, Clients & Mailing Lists

Networking has become an "art form" in the business world. Business Network International (BNI), for example, has brought businesses together for 24 years, and there may be a chapter near you. www.bni.com If so, you should attend one of their luncheons and introduce yourself. Pass out your business cards. You will be surprised how people will want to know more about your work and how they can help you increase your business.

You, in turn, can help your local businesses to grow also, through referrals and patronage.

When you are attending your local events such as gallery openings and social events, you should feel free to tell people that you are working to increase your contacts and would appreciate their referring clients to you. This is not something that comes easily to most artists, but with a little practice you will become a networking pro! You will be surprised how, when you become more conscious of networking opportunities, you will grow your business.

Have an "open studio" from time to time for some of your business contacts. Local printing companies, designers, architects, framers, builders (they have model homes with walls) and real estate agents should be considered. Expand your circles. It is a win/win situation.

When you have collectors within your locale, they should not only be receiving regular mailings with announcements of your new work, they should be invited to see your work in person in your studio. If you do not have a real "studio," display your new work throughout your home or apartment. Put some on easels.

If having a social event in your own space is impossible, ask a collector or business friend to host a little event for you. Offer to provide refreshments and send out invitations. Give your host or hostess a gift of artwork such as a limited edition print.

In the current economic market, more and more artists are doing this. I have a wonderful friend who designs great jewelry and she has revitalized the home party sales. Tupperware had great success – so can you!

The centerpiece of any marketing effort is lists, lists, lists and more lists. You might consider paying a young person to help you with organizing your program into excel file categories such as collectors, press, potential clients, art consultants, invitation lists to shows, etc. This is a tedious task, but the rewards are worth the trouble.

Your lists should be printable to labels in order to be functional. Your galleries will love you when you give them (on labels) your invitation list to shows. Many galleries will give you names and addresses of people who purchase your artwork, which can be added to your collector list.

Separate email lists are essential to a strong marketing effort. Most email services such as AOL, MSN, etc. have a way of saving your lists into categories. As you know, if you send more than a handful of emails at any time, they will bounce back or get lost in the recipient's spam folder, so you may wish to use an online service such as Constant Contact for your emailing.

www.constantcontact.com has an online demo and free 60-day trial. This is a great tool for emailing galleries an image of your work that links directly to your website. This is a masterful and professional means to stay in touch with your collectors, students, clients, etc. Check it out!

Getting names from art magazines, fellow artists, art organizations, dealers who already sell your work and other art community sources will always be effective. If you are an established artist and experienced at representing yourself you may be ready for targeted mailings.

The return on hard mailings is discouraging and expensive, but email lists can be effective. They will link to your (fabulous) website, where galleries, collectors, art consultants can determine immediately whether your work is of interest. The goal is to have potential clients and art consultants "bookmark" your website, so that when they have clients requesting your type of work, they will have your information readily available.

Membership lists of the American Society of Interior Designers, for example, may be purchased online. http://www.nextmark.com has lists by category of designers and architects. They also have a list of the subscribers to *Hospitality Design Magazine*. You may purchase mailing lists or email lists.

Now is the time to be creative in your approach to mailings. The resources are all there. Don't delay!

"I don't have a lot of respect for talent, Talent is genetic. It's what you do with it that counts."

Martin Rill

"Chance is always powerful. Let your hook be always cast; in the pool where you least expect it, there will be a fish."

Ovid

CHAPTER 12

Make a Plan

Now that you have filed away all this information in your bio-computer, it is time to make a plan. This involves assessing a number of things such as where you are in your career. Are you a recent graduate of art school? Have you been painting for a lifetime and now beginning to market your work? Are you a career artist looking at re-booting your career? Each of these requires a different approach.

Do you have an outlet for your "product" already? Are you wishing to expand your base of operations to include several galleries? Is your work applicable to the hospitality design industry? Are you established locally and wishing to "go national?"

I would encourage you to sit with your notebook and begin to list the kinds of things that can be done (1) immediately (2) in the next several months, and (3) in the next year. Do you need to upgrade your computer, find a helper to input your lists in an orderly fashion and get great photos of all your work? Can you barter some services for a piece of your artwork? Would it be advisable to take a class in Photoshop to gain the skills necessary to create and color correct your images?

Is it time to advertise in your local gallery guide? Is it time to devote some funds to creating a good website?

Is it time to spend some energy getting on those free websites?

Next, make a timeline. Give yourself some deadlines for the tasks that you have already outlined. These are not set in stone, of course, but they will serve to create milestones that are measurable and reachable.

Make a budget. I have always encouraged my artist friends and students to invest in themselves. This is better than the stock market–especially now!

Take a percentage of each piece sold, or each job completed and put toward marketing. For example, if you sell four watercolors this month, you should put a percentage of this toward marketing and allocate some toward more materials, studio expenses, etc.

Artists have a tendency to spend a lot of $$ on materials and next to nothing on promotion. Begin to build a reserve for marketing expenses.

If you are new to the art industry, you will also need to have at least a small budget for creating a good portfolio, getting good photos, creating business cards, and other basics.

It costs nothing to attend gallery openings in your area. It costs nothing to introduce yourself to gallery owners and artists. It is free to make friends who can help you in advancing your career. It costs very little to invite people for coffee to see your new work.

Start small and grow your business. Remember the story of Ralph (Lipschitz) Lauren. One tie at a time!

Index

A

B

C

D

F

M

N

O

P

Q

W

Y

About the Author

Bette Ridgeway is a practicing artist who lives and works in Santa Fe NM. Always an artist, she postponed a full-time art career to raise her family and work in several arts management and fund-raising positions in the Washington DC area.

In the mid-70s she served as Visual Arts Coordinator for the Maryland National Capital Park and Planning Commission, where she applied for and received several National Endowment for the Arts (NEA) and MD State Arts Council grants to advance visual arts programs in the area. She coordinated a federally-funded program which provided working studios for 12 up-and-coming young professional artists. She conducted marketing workshops to provide the young artists with the tools to advance their careers. During her tenure, she worked to obtain funding (both public and private) for the Montpelier Art Center in Laurel MD, and implemented a community art gallery at the Capital Center Arena (now the USAir Arena) in Landover MD - the first art gallery to be established in a sports arena.

As a result of her efforts in Maryland to include disabled individuals in ongoing programs, she was recruited to serve as a Program Director in the newly established National Committee, Arts for the Handicapped, an educational affiliate of the John F. Kennedy Center for the Performing Arts. Within a short period of time, she was appointed CEO and President of the non-profit where she developed several model projects and curriculum for disabled students in response to the passage of Public Law-94142 (which guaranteed the rights of students—including disabled young people—to a free, appropriate education).

Under the leadership of Jean Kennedy Smith and an active Board of Directors, Chaired by Dr. Ernest L. Boyer (CEO of the Carnegie Foundation for the Advancement of Teaching),

Ridgeway coordinated a national program that brought music, art, dance and drama to 36 million disabled children and youth. These programs were designed not only to develop artistic skills, but also to be a vehicle for learning basic skills such as math and reading.

Following her work with VSA, she was recruited by Dr. Ray S. Cline, former Deputy Director for Intelligence at the CIA. Cline led a Soviet Studies Project at Georgetown University's prominent think tank, the Center for Strategic and International Studies (CSIS). She assisted Dr. Cline for several years in raising funds for his many projects including the National Intelligence Studies Center. She was recruited by CSIS in 1985 to serve as Deputy Director of Development for CSIS.

While working in these demanding careers, the artist pursued her painting part-time and had a few successful exhibitions. During her tenure as Executive Director of Very Special Arts, she met internationally recognized artist, Paul Jenkins. Jenkins understood the importance of incorporating the visual arts into the curriculum of disabled young people and served as a volunteer, conducting several workshops throughout the US.

When Jenkins saw Ridgeway's modest watercolors he generously took the time to critique her work. At the time, the artist was producing colorful landscapes and seascapes. Jenkins acknowledged that she was a colorist by nature and urged her to eliminate subject matter, to work larger and to focus on color, space and light. Taking his advice, she spent the next 25 years developing her own artistic vocabulary.

In 1996 she moved to Santa Fe, where she has pursued a professional career where she has honed her technical skills and put to use her well-developed marketing skills.

In Santa Fe, the artist has shown in several prominent galleries and owned Ridgeway Gallery at 702 Canyon Road, Santa Fe

1997-1999. She served as Director of Henington Gallery 2001-2001 and Andreeva Gallery and Portrait Academy 2006-2007.

Since 2003 Ridgeway has been represented by galleries in Santa Fe NM, Fort Worth TX, Wilmington NC, Sedona AZ, Richmond VA and Sarasota FL.

In addition to being a full-time painter, she has developed a web design business, custom jewelry design business and in September 2009 will launch Ridgeway Editions, a boutique fine art publishing house.

The author may be reached at bridgesfnm@aol.com.